LETTING GO of Your
PAST

LETTING GO of Your
PAST

JOHN LOREN & PAULA SANDFORD

Charisma
HOUSE
A STRANG COMPANY

Letting Go of Your Past by John Loren and Paula Sandford
Published by Charisma House
A Strang Company
600 Rinehart Road
Lake Mary, Florida 32746
www.charismahouse.com

Cover Designer: Justin Evans
Executive Design Director: Bill Johnson

Library of Congress Cataloging-in-Publication Data:

Sandford, John Loren.
  Letting go of your past / John Loren & Paula Sandford.
    p. cm.
  ISBN 978-1-59979-218-7
  1. Spiritual healing. 2. Interpersonal relations--Religious aspects--Christianity. I. Sandford, Paula. II. Title.
  BT732.5.S228 2008
  248.4--dc22

                              2007034240

Portions of this book were previously published as *The Transformation of the Inner Man* by John and Paula Sandford, copyright © 1982 by Victory House, Inc., ISBN 0-932081-13-4; and *Healing the Wounded Spirit* by John and Paula Sandford, copyright © 1985 by Victory House, Inc., ISBN 0-932081-14-2.

08 09 10 11 12 — 987654321
Printed in the United States of America

CONTENTS

INTRODUCTION

Throughout the world, in many nations and their cultures, two drastic mistakes are being made that did not happen so much in previous centuries. The first has to do with education and training. We rightly will not allow a medical doctor to practice without years of stringent training, passing tough tests, and undergoing further training in internships. That's an interesting word—*practice*. Thank God physicians must become experts in their field before being allowed to "practice" on us! Lawyers must study for years and pass the bar. Architects must study until they understand stresses, lest buildings collapse. Dentists cannot fill or pull teeth until learning has made them capable and we acknowledge that is so. And so it goes for nearly every field of human endeavor. But for the most important occupations of all, being married and raising children, we demand no training whatsoever—and then wonder what went wrong!

This was not so in biblical days. The home was held in highest esteem as the center of training for all of life. One can see it throughout the Bible: "These words, which I am commanding you today, shall be on your heart; and you shall teach them diligently to your sons" (Deut. 6:6–7). "Hear, O sons, the instruction of a father, and give attention that you may gain understanding, for I give you sound teaching; do not abandon my instruction. When I was a son to my father, tender and the only son in the sight of my mother, then he taught me and said to me, 'Let your heart hold fast my words; keep my commandments and live'" (Prov. 4:1–4).

Observe that keeping our father's commandments is to result in *life*, the inference being that failing to do so results in death, which we see all around us and in every morning newspaper. "Fathers, do not provoke your children to anger; but bring them up in the discipline and instruction of the Lord" (Eph. 6:4). In this book and in our other writings, you will learn how, since the Industrial Revolution of the 1840s, family roles, especially those of fathers, have been progressively more and more destroyed, with one of the most harmful results being that children becoming adults are no longer disciplined and trained by their fathers and mothers in the arts of marriage and child raising. So, though in every other field people are carefully prepared, young adults are cast woefully ignorant upon the two most critical occupations of all!

This book is one, among many, that attempts to address that lack. You will find teachings about how to reparent those who were not equipped in their childhood and how to be yourself reparented. This book provides lessons on what teenage problems are, cutting free from parents as adults in righteous and wholesome ways, what parental inversion and substitute spouse are, how to find the right spouse, how to find and become your destiny, and how to become one with others in unity in the body of Christ. No young adult should enter the fields of marriage and parenting without training, which he or she can get from this book and many others, such as our book *Restoring the Christian Family*.

Another grievous error is that people are let loose upon society—and their own lives—with little or no healing to the wounds in their past, from their own sins or parental failures and sins during their childhood. How strange it is that we will not let professional athletes become members of a team without careful medical exams, and if there are dangerous wounds yet unhealed, we disqualify them from playing, but we do not apply the same common sense to our young people before marriage and parenthood! There are no laws that require counsel and prayer before marriage. Jeremiah said, "The heart is more deceitful than all else and is desperately sick" (Jer. 17:9), and Jesus said, "For out of the heart come evil thoughts, murders, adulteries, fornications, thefts, false witness, slanders" (Matt. 15:19). Yet we remain stubbornly ignorant of what is in our hearts and more unaware how to heal so that our marriages and child raising could have opportunity to produce blessing rather than harm. Divorce rates, violence, and murder run rampant in our society. This book is one of many Paula and I have written to instruct the body of Christ how to transform the heart from evil consequences to joyous living in Christ. You will learn how to let go of and be healed of the wounds from the past, how to crucify coping practices that bring harm, and then how to resurrect the heart to become whom God intended, until all become maturely one in the body of Christ.

In previous centuries, preaching and teaching called more directly and powerfully for repentance and change. People knew that if they received Jesus as their Lord and Savior, their lives had to change accordingly. The first and second Great Awakenings in America transformed lives and much of society, even the unbelieving. But we have feasted on cheap grace and what Jesus, like our own personal Santa Claus, will do for us. Previous generations heard the claims of Christ upon their lives. Our recent generations have been raised on what claims we have upon Him. The result has been too little real repentance and change. This book, along with others, calls for real repentance and for moral rectitude—not religiously or in condemnation, but letting go of the past—applying the blood, cross, and resurrection of our Lord

Jesus Christ to the depths of the heart, knowing that it is the kindness of God that leads to true repentance (Rom. 2:4).

We, the whole body of Christ, must learn how to be true physicians of the heart, one to another. "Speaking the truth in love, we are to grow up in all aspects into Him, who is the head, even Christ" (Eph. 4:15).

CHAPTER 1

GROWING UP
AGAIN—IN CHRIST

"Before she travailed, she brought forth; before her pain
came, she gave birth to a boy. Who has heard such a
thing? Who has seen such things? Can a land be born in
one day? Can a nation be brought forth all at once? As
soon as Zion travailed, she also brought forth her sons.
Shall I bring to the point of birth, and not give delivery?"
says the LORD. "Or shall I who gives delivery shut the
womb?" says your God. "Be joyful with Jerusalem and
rejoice for her, all you who love her; be exceedingly
glad with her, all you who mourn over her, that you
may nurse and be satisfied with her comforting breasts,
that you may suck and be delighted with her bountiful
bosom." For thus says the LORD, "Behold I extend peace
to her like a river, and the glory of the nations like an
overflowing stream; and you shall be nursed, you shall
be carried on the hip and fondled on the knees. As one
whom his mother comforts, so I will comfort you; and
you shall be comforted in Jerusalem."

—ISAIAH 66:7–13

Why can I progress only so far with you, John? I just know I can't become any more whole with you. What's missing?" That drove me to see that so long as I lived too much for my image of myself as a prayer minister, no one could really become free (of me or self or anything else) because I needed that person to be sick so I could help him. But when the Holy Spirit revealed the many ego trips—that I needed to help someone, to be "one up" on someone by being "more whole" than the other, to center on problems, to martyr myself for the other, and so on—then He revealed that none or all of those sinful propensities put together answered the question. Something else was missing.

He made me aware that it was not enough merely to bring the sinful side of man to the cross. The person to whom I ministered could discover every sinful deed and carry every practice to the cross and still remain a functionally incapable person! *I knew then that more important than death to the negative is resurrection of the other to new life.* The first must happen before the second, but without resurrection, a person is little helped. When we have forgiven those who failed us or have been forgiven of all judgments, but we have not received enough human love, we may still be unable to function wholesomely. Someone must love us back to life! Sometimes God sovereignly does so, by Himself, but most often human hands and hearts are needed to touch and draw us forward into life.

After being born anew, we are, in fact, babies again. As God did not design us like fish, to be hatched physically without natural father or mother, so He never intended that we should be reborn spiritually without the nurture of a family. That fact alone is sufficient reason for our being born anew within the Church, but it is also perhaps the least understood fact of our Christian existence. Somehow we have failed to understand our importance to one another.

JOHN'S STORY OF LETTING GO AND GROWING UP

There was a time during my ministry when people had a hard time becoming whole when I ministered to them. It never entered my head that they needed my personal love in any more special way than generally as a Christian or any more uniquely than as a friend and prayer minister. The Lord revealed to me that some people in my and Paula's care needed us to give ourselves to them as a spiritual father or mother. Lacking this kind of relationship, they could not come to fullness of life.

I had puzzled, "Why are people latching onto Paula and me inappropriately? Is there something in our flesh that wrongly attracts?" The more we tried to avoid it, the more people drained our energies. Then the Lord spoke in His still, small voice: "John, the reason they continue to latch onto you and Paula (after you have died to all the wrong things in you) is that your presence promises something you are withholding. Paradoxically, if you will open up and give all of yourselves, they will be satisfied, and they will not drain you anymore."

He went on to explain that what they wanted was not something they should not want; even in the cases in which some would try to seduce us sexually if they thought they could, that was not actually what they wanted. What some people actually were seeking was what they had never received—the wholesome love of parents by which to come to life. If we would offer ourselves (as in Romans 12:1) to the Father as a vehicle for His love, He would so satisfy their hearts that not only would they not drain us, but also they would become whole.

When I finally realized this was something the Father God wanted to do and that He needed willing human hearts to accomplish it, Paula and I moved past the fear of doing something scripturally wrong and saw that the work is indeed scriptural. (See 1 Thessalonians 2:11–12; 1 Timothy 1:2.) The Holy Spirit then overcame our fears of risking ourselves too much, showing us that the work is really that of the Father, so we began to let Him do it in and through us. We opened up and began to say in prayer aloud with the people to whom we ministered:

> *Insofar as [the person needing ministry] needs a father and mother to bring him to life, and will accept us for a while as parents in Christ, we will be that, dear Lord. We will carry [name of person] in our hearts and let You love him [or her] to life.*

Results were immediate and astonishing. People began to be able to take hold of their lives and grow up more quickly. Because we let go of our need to be needed and began to trust God to make them whole through us, the burden was easier for us to bear, not heavier as we had feared. Perhaps consciously accepting the burden helped. Or maybe the ending of our resistance made us more transparent (not less as we had feared), and people could obtain what they needed from God more easily and quickly through us.

I began to see then that here was another key to the kingdom that had been lost to God's people. We need to be more aware of our need for one another. We must not become so lost from what "church" is that we become confined to what is only the temple—the location where individuals come to worship as individuals and go home the same way, minus the corporate life of the Church. We had been afraid of the verse, "And do not call anyone on earth your father; for One is your Father, He who is in heaven" (Matt. 23:9). Those words were mainly to keep the Jews from idolizing ancestors, specifically Abraham. (See John 8:39.) (Christians do need to remember this verse as a warning against idolizing those who love us to life.) Consequently, we missed, or were blinded, to those scriptures that appear many times in the writings of St. Paul.

> For in Christ Jesus I became your father through the gospel.
> —1 CORINTHIANS 4:15

> For although you may have ten thousand others to teach you about Christ, remember that you have only me as your father.
> —1 CORINTHIANS 4:15, TLB

> But you know of his proven worth that he served with me in the furtherance of the gospel like a child serving his father.
> —PHILIPPIANS 2:22

> Just as you know how we were exhorting and encouraging and imploring each one of you as a father would his own children, so that you may walk in a manner worthy of the God who calls you into His own kingdom and glory.
> —1 THESSALONIANS 2:11–12

The Church must be strong in its ability to rise to its glory (Isa. 60:1–2). We have to first let go of the negative and take it to the cross. Then we need to resurrect one another to life. First Thessalonians 2:7–8 says, "But we proved to be gentle among you, as a nursing mother tenderly cares for her own children. Having thus a fond affection for you, we were well-pleased to impart to you not only the gospel of God but also our own lives, because you had become very dear to us."

That text does not speak of the children of our physical wombs but of the womb of Christ: "My children, with whom I am again in labor until Christ is formed in you" (Gal. 4:19). St. Paul is speaking of labor pains; he is pregnant with their spiritual life, "because I have you in my heart" (Phil. 1:7).

Once we have been birthed, we need to be raised as sons and daughters in Christ. "Whosoever shall not [become willing to] receive the kingdom of God as a little child, he shall not enter therein" (Mark 10:15, KJV). Some, not knowing, have unconsciously reached out of hearts of love and accomplished that rearing for one another without naming it as such. People say, "My, what a loving church. You can feel it when you walk in." But how much better would it be if we could recognize the need to be raised and to raise one another and respond knowingly, aware of the pitfalls, trained in the artistry of it? Truly, "My people go into exile for their lack of knowledge; and their honorable men are famished, and their multitude is parched with thirst" (Isa. 5:13). Successful spiritual parenting is a key to helping us grow up in Christ. It is also a key in helping us to let go of past inclinations, strongholds, and besetting sins. As new foundations are built through spiritual parenting, many countless Christians can be kept from leading faltering lives.

FOR THOSE CALLED TO BE SPIRITUAL PARENTS

Not everyone needs spiritual parenting. Some, usually those whose parents were affectionate, attentive, and wise, received so much naturally that when they were born anew, God the Father was able to immediately and easily parent them to fullness in their new lives because of that blessed relationship they had with their earthly parents. Such people easily drink from their pastor and from more mature friends in the body and grow from them, without having to enter more specifically and consciously into spiritual parenting.

We cannot parent everyone we meet. How do we know when God calls us specifically to this or that person either to parent or to be parented? First, one learns to recognize it in the heart. Somehow a person "knows" this one is "in my bag." One comes to recognize that the feelings of the spirit and the position granted are not merely as a friend or as a brother or sister, but that of a father or mother. We need then to talk about it openly and directly. We never insist where the relationship is unwanted—even if we know that is what the other actually needs. The other must welcome the relationship, whether to be the one to parent or to be parented.

We can learn by experience to recognize the signs of need and, by more experience, to question whether someone else is a more likely candidate to fulfill this role. Then we wait upon the Lord for confirmation.

No one can tell at the beginning of a spiritual parenting relationship how much will be required. Some people, though badly starved by their natural parents, nevertheless drink easily and quickly from the Lord and the body of Christ and rise to maturity in a short while. Some, raised by wonderful parents, take years of conscious spiritual parenting to mature. Each person is unique and has within him his own agenda and timetable. Hard-and-fast rules will not fit every person. No one ought to be praised or blamed for either quickness or slowness in maturing. People are simply different. We need to be prepared to be continually sensitive to the Holy Spirit and to people to see when and where we are in the process of their maturation.

When we offer ourselves to spiritually parent another, a range of varying experiences may occur. We carry the other in our hearts. Therefore, we may feel in our own body and heart what the other person endures. We may know his or her loneliness, fear, insecurity, anger, doubt, oppression, and so on because we identify and experience it in ourselves. Sometimes we may think that some negative thing we experience is our own trouble before we realize it is the other's, or our spiritual child's joy may well up in our own breast.

I know this feeling personally. The Lord so unites me with the other and so lays his welfare into my heart that if I do not see that person for a while, I know experientially what St. Paul meant when he wrote, "When we could endure it no longer...we sent Timothy, our brother and God's fellow worker in the gospel of Christ, to strengthen and encourage you as to your faith" (1 Thess. 3:1–2). When I come into that person's city again and see him or her, my spirit leaps up with joy, and just as he is refreshed, I am refreshed.

Strangely, when that person hugs me or drinks greedily from me, I am not wearied; I am refreshed. It is as though I am being allowed to fulfill a calling. Consciously knowing and talking things out eases my heart. I know then what my spirit has been grappling with in the darkness. But when a child in Christ thinks to protect me from his problems (not because of growing maturity but from the flesh) and fails to share, I am stuck with his nameless mess. I wrestle in the dark, and the burden of that child becomes unnecessarily heavy. Like a natural parent, I become anxious to know what is going on. I may press and wrestle not to invade or coerce the other to share too much too soon.

In initial stages, Paula and I want to see that person often, as parents must spend more time forming an infant's character. Once a week at least we need to talk together, and the relationship is colored mostly by teaching and prayer. As the need arises, we might find ourselves informally applying prayer ministry regarding root issues. However, if it turns out that a spiritual son or daughter needs structured, ongoing prayer ministry, it would be best to have someone else fill that role. Later, when major problems are worked through and a fullness of bond with us is established, that maturing child may not need so much proximity. The union of our spirits can conquer time and space, needing only occasional renewal. As time progresses, so does weaning, until the result is much the same as with a mature natural child—friendship flavored by the residue that a parent remains always a parent, though also a companion. My natural children correct me and advise me, but they always do so with the deference and respect due their father. So it is with God's children.

Some I misjudged and tried to release too soon, with resultant cries of pain. Later Paula and I learned to let maturation and release happen as naturally as it does with our own progeny. Each one matures and cuts free in his own timetable and in his own way, some easily and some with difficulty. Parents in Christ need to learn to ride the waves as they come, not becoming too upset if one thinks he must become angry or another thinks he must compete and win in order to cut spiritual umbilical cords. Once one understands what the other is actually accomplishing, the way he does it can be taken impersonally and with equanimity.

FOR THOSE WHO ARE CONSIDERING
SPIRITUAL PARENTING

If you are considering becoming a spiritual father or mother, we advise you to first examine yourself. Do you need this to give you an identity? Does calling yourself someone's spiritual parent flatter you? Does it make you feel important? If you give out of your own need, it will be all too easy to turn adult spiritual children into actual children and rob them of the very maturity you are aiming to install.

Is your home life stable? How are you doing at raising your own children? Paul advised Timothy that a pastor "must manage his own family well and see that his children obey him with proper respect. (If anyone does not know how to manage his own family, how can he take care of God's church?)" (1 Tim. 3:4–5, NIV). Although a spiritual parent is not a pastor, we believe he should apply the same standards to himself, for he assists his pastor in the task of shepherding a soul. Paul went on to say a pastor must not be a recent convert (v. 6). Neither should a spiritual parent, for a newborn babe cannot take care of others. Have you had time to mature? What do those who know you say about all this? Seek discernment from friends who are unafraid to confront you, especially your pastor and other elders. Or are you even under authority? How then can you place a spiritual child under your own authority?

Will the task of spiritual parenting leave enough time for your own children? If it does, will there be enough time left over for your spiritual son or daughter? (Most have been neglected before; you must guard against wounding them again.) Finally, does the spiritual son or daughter really want healing and growth, or just to be taken care of? Remember, your task is to facilitate the maturing process, not enable dependency.

FOR THOSE WHO NEED SPIRITUAL REPARENTING

If you are one who needs spiritual parenting, our advice is to observe how your prospective parents in Christ have related with their natural children. Unfortunately, some spiritual parents have been possessive, domineering, cold, controlling, and so on with their own children. And the Lord may not yet have transformed them in many of those areas. From such comes blaspheming of the entire work, until some fear to venture at all. If you observe that your prospective spiritual parents' children are rebellious and angry or controlled and immature, find someone else! Steer clear! Unless mighty works of grace have progressed, such a person will most likely make the same mistakes with you! On the other hand, if the adult children or the children who remain in the home relate easily and with humor, fondness, and respect, you will most likely be able to do so also.

Look well to the home life before you commit yourself. Unless the need is severe, and you and your spiritual parents are exceptionally stable and other mature, discerning Christians have deemed living together advisable, you will not live in the home and will visit only occasionally. In any case, the practices built in the home by which offspring relate to parents, and vice versa, will be those you will be blessed by or will have to wrestle with. Fathers and mothers in Christ who are filled with wisdom, grace, and stature are to be cherished, as there are all too few "safe" ones in the body of Christ.

If failure with our own children is what mellows, humbles, and prepares us to be good fathers and mothers in Christ, how then shall we know whether prospective parents whose children may still be rebellious though the parents may have changed and matured have, in fact, been crucified and changed? By their fruits. Look to the other present relationships. How do they relate to friends? If he is a boss, how do subordinates react to him? If she is a leader, how do followers relate to her? Even so, entering a more primal relationship may dig into areas that secondary relationships do not touch, so be prepared to risk, and gain, whatever God will teach. Once we have let God write on our hearts what He intends, He can lead us to graduate to another class and another teacher (or parent) if need be, or perhaps to none, maturation having arrived. My first two fathers in Christ both tumbled and fell, but the Lord blessed me through those imperfect vessels anyway.

When It Is Time to Let Go

When maturity calls for closure, or when it is time to fly from the nest, perhaps to another or never to need another, one feels it deep inside. What the "parent" says no longer touches the heart as needed revelation; it bounces off our own sturdy realizations as unnecessary, perhaps as being even redundant. We no longer need proximity. We feel complete and secure alone, in whatever circumstance. "Well, what do you know? I handled that rather easily. I would have blown up before." "Hey, that situation didn't frighten me like it used to." "I didn't feel like I needed advice; I could trust my own wisdom there—how about that!" "I don't feel unloved anymore." "People don't bother me like they used to."

"I didn't get addled like I would have before—I'm stronger." In short, we just don't feel like we need parenting in the same way anymore. Running back for counsel now seems more like a cop-out than a help. We want now to sit down and visit and maybe share our new discoveries, but we feel "put down" and "missed" if the parent in Christ returns to the old way of ministering. It becomes insulting. We are beyond that, and if we still retain a need, it is for that "parent" to see our freedom and relate to us as mature equals.

There may still be times when we will want to return to "check in" or to receive guidance about another specific problem. It is a mark of maturity when we feel the freedom to do that without fear of having to regress to childishness even if the "parent" tries (perhaps inadvertently) to handle us that way. We know then that we are so free, even the one who raised us cannot clip our wings. We can relate all of the above realizations to what we experience when cutting free from our natural parents.

The most important fact of spiritual parenting is simple love and acceptance. Once we, as the "child," realize at deepest heart levels that this is no game, that we really are loved by the Lord through this parent just because we exist; once we feel truly chosen and cherished and settle it that that love is once and for all "given," never to be taken back, security settles in, and healing and maturity flow as the natural outcome. A parent in Christ may fail in countless ways—incapable of understanding at crucial times, inattentive at others, bossy or too demanding, whatever—so long as the love of Jesus Christ flows into our "child's" heart and is received, the primary work is done. From there on we will gain strength to see for ourselves or to overcome wherein we can't see. Ministry from that moment on is the outworking of an accomplished fact of basic wholeness! One could say that this impartation of parental love is *the* basic, simple reason for spiritual parenting. Paula and I have known parents in Christ who totally lacked prayer ministry skills and insights. They were not their "children's" counselors, advisors, or teachers. They hardly ever said a word. They were merely present and available, as hug blankets. And the "children" matured beautifully.

The Necessity of the Spiritual Extended Family

Natural nuclear families suffer when isolated. We need grandparents, uncles, aunts, and cousins. Part of America's mounting problems—not only in the nuclear family from divorce rates, adulteries, and such, but also in increasing criminal activity, drugs, unproductiveness at work, and so on—can be traced in part to increased mobility that has destroyed interfamily relationships. Nuclear families need the support, refreshment, and counsel of blood relatives and close friends. Extended family relationships and parental relationships in Christ need this support also.

Parents in Christ need the fullness of the church family about them. Worship refreshes and strengthens the heart to hold itself open. The Word of God revives the soul and instructs. Pastors and friends share and counsel. Fellow parents in Christ can compare notes.

Sometimes children in Christ can be part of the same body, which is preferable, but sometimes not. Time and space or other conditions may prevent. Paula and I never have asked that a Roman Catholic child in Christ attend any church but a Catholic church—or for that matter that any child in Christ attend our own church. In such cases, we encourage each child in Christ to be regular in attendance in whatever church he has membership. Both "parents" and "children" need the blessing of the body of Christ.

Brothers and sisters in Christ are part of the parcel. Sometimes the local church fills the need. Sometimes friends fill this need, quite apart from the parents. But usually our children in Christ recognize a kinship in one another and delight to visit. That sense of belonging also helps to build security, even if sibling rivalries become part of the scenario. Who better to wrestle with and learn from than a brother or sister in a family? As battling siblings usually mature into close friends, so do children in Christ. Sibling rivalries are nothing to fear, even as wise natural parents chuckle, mediate, and wait for maturity.

GROWING UP IN CHRIST

Parent-child relationships in Christ are far more temporary than the natural. Sometimes acceptance is the single touch needed, and in a matter of weeks the person is whole and free. Often, our experience is that spiritual parenting requires about two to three years. Depending on the degree of need and the person's own developmental timetable, the "child" has matured through childish ways to adolescence to maturity within that time.

One person who was being spiritually parented, more perceptive than most, could quite accurately assess her own spiritual age. One day she came in and said, "I'm about six emotionally now, aren't I?" In most ways to outsiders she might have appeared quite mature and free. But in her primary relationships with her own immediate family she was accurate. Later she announced, "I'm a teenager now, aren't I?" And she was right. In a few months she was mature and free.

When I was a child, I used to speak as a child, think as a child, reason as a child; when I became a man, I did away with childish things.

—1 CORINTHIANS 13:11

A parent in Christ has one fundamental task: to impart such love and strength to his or her spiritual children that they are empowered to "do away" or let go of childish things. Note the "I" in the verse—*I* grow up, *I* put away childish ways. Herein lies perhaps the most crucial guideline for parents in Christ: we must not try to grow the other up; that's the child's task and God's job in their heart. Though a person may regress and relate sometimes childishly to us, we always treat the other as the adult he is. When we give affection, we know we are reaching to the part of the heart that has not matured beyond childhood. When we pray aloud with them, we consciously and intentionally reach that place in the heart. But in all other aspects of the relationship we are careful to treat the other with full respect as an adult. We can enter reparenting and err drastically by reducing grown people to children.

SPIRITUAL PARENTING PITFALLS

Pitfalls abound in spiritual parenting. Some friends of ours had to give up on a girl who came to live with them because she would not stop projecting her parental expectations upon them and consequently would not stop rebelling against what she only thought they felt and meant. Parents in Christ may (sometimes unwittingly) unplug inner volcanoes that have nowhere to come out but on them. Children in Christ may need to express love and receive touches of love so much that outsiders may think wrongly of the relationship—"Did you see the way that young girl looks at him? You'd think he'd know better!" "Is Mary aware of the way that young man hangs around her? His intentions can't be right or he wouldn't be hanging around her like he does!" Parents must be so secure as to be able to withstand gossips and maligners without being ruffled. And here is where wise pastors and elders need to protect those who reparent others in their congregations. A word from a pastor can quench smoldering fires.

A wise proverb says, "If you find a man of wisdom, let your foot wear out his threshold." Children sometimes want to latch on and spend inordinate amounts of time just soaking up the family atmosphere. Sometimes that ought to be allowed, and sometimes it gets out of hand. Parents need to exercise discernment carefully about this, so as to open the home fully at some times with some such children in Christ and tactfully draw lines and limits at other times.

Spiritual children either in the home or frequently visiting can become a blessing to natural children. Our six children have all been blessed and matured by being part of our ministry to others. But we were careful to watch that our own children's time and attention were not given too much to others. One man and wife we knew had had too many foster children in the home for too many years. Their children felt neglected and left out, and their own space and time with each other had been invaded too much and had been lost. The home life was disrupted, and tension and battles rent the peace of the home every day. It is not wisdom to take on so much that there is no healthy home life left to impart. Natural children's God-given right to peace and joy in their own home must not be sacrificed.

Some spiritual children have had no other experience in their own childhood home than to compete with siblings. Some siblings lied, cheated, and stole. Some were seductive both to the parents and/or to siblings. Some were loud and boisterous. Some taught wrong things. Some enticed others to immoral, reckless, or inconsiderate actions. Thus, a spiritual child might have dysfunctional ways of relating to his spiritual parents' natural children. Parents must be alert to protect their children—in body, heart, and mind. The struggle can help parents, as their own children see and discuss wrong examples, in training their children in right ways. But when and if too many forces impinge on the home, parents must hold their calling to raise their own in security as their absolute first priority.

Not all spiritual parenting is successful, and we need to be sensitive to the guidance of the Lord, directly and through pastors and friends, when He sometimes says, "Hang in there; you are not a hireling who flees" (see John 10:13), and at other times when He may say, "Quitting is not flight; it is merely wisdom to admit that this attempt isn't working out."

As each of us comes closer to the core rottenness and thus to the depth of real, life-changing repentance, we approach levels of fear heretofore unknown. One pastor friend and his wife entered into a small group with Paula and me. As the Holy Spirit began to reach to the pastor's inner core, he said, "I don't believe I am going to like what I see." At the depths of us all is sinfulness so evil it cannot be healed; it can only be slain.

One way of viewing the Book of Revelation is to see that it can also be a parable of our interior life. Once one confronts his inner depths, he knows that whatever "beast" may be out there, his first battle is with his own inner beast. He takes home to his own heart such scriptures (Rev. 13–21) as a parable of his own interior Armageddon. (This is not to say there is not an exterior "beast," "Armageddon," or the like—only that the wise know there is a parallel in their own hearts.)

This pastor saw the beginning depths of the battle and fled. Subsequently, since he had refused to listen to the kind messenger (the Holy Spirit), a pharisaical, false, holiness teaching took hold of him and his church and cost him his pastorate. The same flight may happen in spiritual parent-child relationships.

When parents in Christ discern flight mechanisms developing, they need to pray strength into their spiritual child (Eph. 3:16) and then to confront them. Needless to say, tact is paramount. There is no guarantee a parent will be able to keep a child from fleeing. We could not keep that pastor from fleeing from the depths of himself, though we tried everything we knew to do. Parents need to have "see-through" faith for their children in such cases. We need to be able to hold in our heart the faith that though our loved one has not chosen the safe road, God will teach him the hard way, and he will come out wiser in the end. It is important to know when to let go—even as we had to learn to let our natural children learn the hard way and as the father of the prodigal son had to let him go.

Spiritual parenting in Christ is dissimilar to natural parenting in this dimension: that in it God is not merely raising a child, as He is in natural homes, but He may also be digging to the depth of transformation. There is a depth of transformation that not all enter. Some call it the "wilderness experience"; some call it "the long dark night of the soul." We wrote of it in *The Elijah Task*, pages 46–50.[1] Even though all Christians are chosen (1 Pet. 2:9; Eph. 1:3–5), only a few respond to enter such depths.

If you have felt this urgency to dig to the depths of your soul, you may be in a regrowth process. You will require a spiritual parent to be perceptive and to stand by longer in the process, letting it happen. It is especially important that parents in Christ know when you are entering that time of shattering and brokenness reserved for only those whom God receives for fullness. You will require paradoxically different treatment than other children in Christ. This is not the time for you to be palliated, overcomforted, helped too much, counseled too much, or expected to perform outwardly as competently as others or even as you previously could. Neither pity nor sympathy will help you at all. This is a private desert of death, and it needs to be so. But paradoxically you will need parents to stand by you more than others who may not be going through such throes. You will need precisely and only that—your parents standing by. It will be a comfort to you, while everything else is in interior flux, that your parents in Christ are standing, merely there, not changing, not doing anything but being something of calm permanence that does not change.

Parents then fulfill Galatians 6:2 at its highest. They bear what the one being crucified cannot bear, even as the Father sent an angel to strengthen Jesus in the garden (Luke 22:43). They stand by quietly believing when you can't believe for yourself anymore. They hope when the worm in the chrysalis has lost hope. They endure whatever flip-flops and hurts you go through, saying nothing. It is important in such situations that parents in Christ know to say nothing, only to be there, for whatever they impart will only postpone you from entering fullness. You must find for yourself, or the wilderness does not accomplish its full purpose. Parents must know then not to teach and advise as they would another not so engaged. They must only stand and watch, knowing that watching is far from inactive; it is love at its fullest. (We would like to protect ourselves from the suffering of it by getting the other through it faster and easier, but true love knows it must not.)

SINGLE PARENTS IN CHRIST

Sometimes those who are single—never married, widowed, or divorced—find themselves called to be parents in Christ, sometimes for persons chronologically older than themselves. In the Roman Catholic Church, priests and appointed laypeople have long been "spiritual directors" (a position much akin to spiritual parenting). Since it is the Father who accomplishes, and since we have all had experience being raised in natural families, of course the unmarried, even the never married, can raise children in Christ, although no one can advise married couples who are parents better than a married parent. It would be far better if the prayer minister or spiritual parent were married and a parent, but if a person knows that he or she is called to minister as a parent and is not married or a parent, then the lack in this area need not prevent him or her from doing what God has ordained. God can impart wisdom. Not having a mate also leaves the prayer minister vulnerable, but that also is regularly overcome, for example, by fathers and nuns in the Roman Catholic Church. Though we could all point to instances of seduction or failure, so could we in cases of married prayer ministers. In short, though married parents have a natural head start in prayer ministry and reparenting, no single person should feel disqualified or second-class—it is God who accomplishes.

As love is the cornerstone of reparenting, transparency is its touchstone. We shall know whether success has been attained not only by the signs of maturity given earlier but also primarily by one distinction: Has the person reached through to Jesus? Is he closer to Him than he was before (Phil. 3:7–10)? Does he know and cherish Jesus more, or less? Is his walk in Him stronger and freer?

Natural maturity is fine, but we want foremost growth in Christ. Is he into the Word more? Does he attend church more faithfully? Has he engaged in viable ministry in Christ? Is he seeking the Lord more zealously? Is his devotional life more tender and full?

It is the Word of God that causes growth in Christ. "Like newborn babes, long for the pure milk of the word, that by it you may grow in respect to salvation" (1 Pet. 2:2). Prayer ministers and parents in Christ only adjust that growth (Eph. 4:11–12). We do not cause growth. God does, mainly through His Word. We must be careful never to replace God in attention, affection, or whatever is happening. The other must be kept free first to relate to God Himself. We stand by. Only that.

CHAPTER 2

YOU ARE NOT YOUR PARENTS' FATHER OR MOTHER

The father of the righteous will greatly rejoice, and he who begets a wise son will be glad in him. Let your father and your mother be glad, and let her rejoice who gave birth to you.

—PROVERBS 23:24–25

And, fathers, do not provoke your children to anger; but bring them up in the discipline and instruction of the Lord.

—EPHESIANS 6:4

Parental inversion is our term to describe what happens whenever one or both parents are so immature or ineffective that a child takes responsibility to parent his parent(s). That inverts God-given order. Part of each parent's task is to provide a secure home in which a child can be free to be a child. Parents are to care for children, not the other way around. Chores and responsibilities are good training for children, but the weight of care and responsibility for the family should rest on the parents' shoulders, never on the children. Likewise, it is good for children to learn to love and bless parents, but parents should not burden children with the role of comforter and confidant. Wherever this inversion or substitution has crept into our lives, we have to identify these issues from our past and let them go in order for us to move into the glory God has for us.

We have observed that children today have too often been made to feel useless. The more our labor-saving devices have done away with previously necessary household chores, the less our children have been given the opportunity to learn life's greatest secret— that happiness belongs to those who have learned to lay down their lives in service to others. Consequently, it has not been easy for some to see that parental inversion is harmful. People to whom we have ministered often report with pride and joy how in their childhood they took hold when their family needed them. That's all well and good; it's far better that trouble should arrive by the route of a child's overserving than that failure happen by selfish unwillingness. Nevertheless, sin is involved, and we need to help people see it in order to set them free.

The heart is never pure no matter how noble the service. No matter how pleased all concerned may be that a member of the family has been helpful, and no matter how much our Lord wants to reward us for trying to honor our parents by serving, the sin side of our actions still demands reaping until transformation by the cross sets us free. God sent the Son that He may reward the servant and prevent destruction. "For God is not unjust so as to forget your work and the love which you have shown toward His name, in having ministered and in still ministering to the saints" (Heb. 6:10).

Insofar as parental inversion is sin, it has as its base disrespect for parents who fail. It is good if a child tries to honor and respect his parents, but none can keep the heart completely free from disappointment, hurt, judgment, resentment, and disrespect. Whether a parent fails in place or by being absent, it is almost impossible for the child to avoid the sin of usurpation. He is taking over functions that belong to another; thus he is in the position of usurpation, whether intended or not. Nor is it altogether possible to avoid the sin of not trusting God. Parents color God to children, so whether consciously or unconsciously, the child's picture of God begins to resemble the failing parent(s). From then on the child may not be able to trust in reality in the heart that God is on His throne. "The world will fall apart," if the child doesn't hold it together.

Parental inversion robs a child of his childhood. It builds into children inability to rest. It rapes rest from then on. Parents provide security, but when parents fight or the home is filled with unspoken tensions between them, one or more children may take responsibility to try to hold them together. Once that stance is established in the heart, a child may manifest that fear-filled attempt to hold life together inappropriately everywhere. Such an adult cannot let people fight things out healthily—"Oh, I just can't stand it when people fight. Let's get this settled." They shush quarrels too soon, unable to trust in healthy dissensions until things can be fully worked through. They may so smooth things over or hold such tight controls that nothing can be fully resolved. They may be compulsive peacemakers, their sin masked behind the beatitude (Matt. 5:9). Others may honor them and so perpetuate their error, not realizing what is really behind their peacemaking.

PI vs. PO With Regard to Parental Inversion

As a person who may have experienced parental inversion (PI) in your home, you may find that you overwork and overachieve much like performance-oriented (PO) people, only from an added wrong motive. Not only is your service to gain acceptance or earn love, but it is also to keep the world of fear and chaos from your door. As a PI person you may become far too busy and may have often said, "Well, I'd rather do it myself." You say this because you are unable to trust that others will hold up their end or do things rightly. Thus you may fall into being a noble martyr, but your stance is actually an unconscious insult to everyone else around you. The insult and put-down come from unconscious anger at your parents for not doing what they should have done. We have all witnessed how some people can be helpful in such a way a person feels honored, while others help in such a bustling, self-martyring way the recipient feels dishonored and insulted. Such are usually PI people.

As a PI person, you cannot rest on vacation or anywhere else. Being a PI person myself, on vacation in a campground, five minutes after arrival I would be wandering around looking for somebody to help—this after a full year of helping people! At home, you learned not to let down your guard for a moment, lest some spontaneous, thoughtless act add one final straw to an already overburdened marriage. As a child you were not free as other children were to be nasty and to experience a little disorder. You were prevented from discovering certain things about yourself by foolishness in the "school of hard knocks." You had to be controlled, but you actually needed self-control to arrive by the slow process of trial and error and inner decision, not from outer compulsion for fear of results in a shaky family.

You may find that you cannot relax and be refreshed in your home. In childhood, your home was identified as the place of tension and consequent demands for emotional responsibility and of attempts to control self and others. It may take some time before you can learn at heart to mature into the reality of "the heart of her husband doth safely trust in her" (Prov. 31:11, kjv). Rest has become identified with solitude or fun and games away from the home. It is a strain and an added discipline of self for you to learn to find rest among the primary people in your life. Initially you are not able to rest in another, because you did not learn to do that in your childhood home. Instead, you find yourself always caring for others, thus effectively holding them at a safe distance from your heart.

Paula was a PO person, but my besetting sin was PI. My father was gone much of the time, and though gentle and kindly, he nevertheless failed greatly to be strong and present more and more as the years wore on. Gradually I assumed more and more responsibility. I became strength for my mother and younger sister and brother. I kept the garden, yard, cows, chickens, orchard, and pets. It was a shock to learn recently that Frank, my brother who is ten years younger than I, had been angry with me because I, as his surrogate father, had left him to go to college. But it was a greater shock to learn very recently that my sister, Martha Jane, only four years younger than I, had been angry with me for identically the same reason. I cried out, "How on earth did I get in that position, dear Lord?" I repented again of usurping my father's position and resigned anew as savior of my family.

God has honored and blessed me in reward for my poor attempts to serve. But there are two sides to every coin. Every symptom listed above, and more, fit me. Now, He is setting me free from compulsive service and from an inability to rest in my home.

God wants to use our Elijah House ministry to help prepare His family for His return, but until I could come to death of my lack of trust in His ability to be head of His family (by projection from untrust of my natural father), no way could my service be untainted by disrespect of His lordship or His fatherhood.

A businessman to whom I had ministered began to discern the source of his striving. His father was a drinker and a gambler. As a lad of eleven, he went to work to earn money for the family. In every way he tried to support his family. From then on he compulsively took care of everyone—employees, friends, wife, children, church, God, anyone, and everything. He was the compulsive good Samaritan for every flat tire and trouble in the way. He could not purchase and enjoy something for himself without inordinate guilt. As a boy he had built into himself that he must give everything to save his family. He could not stop trying—long after the family and everyone else could and should have taken care of themselves.

Worse, his mother had long since learned to control him and pump him for unnecessary services by simply putting him under guilt. He would jump through whatever hoop in order to serve and not fail as his dad had. Not only did business employees milk him for higher-than-normal wages, but also they were ungrateful and attacked him if he couldn't deliver on too extravagant promises. Throughout the healing process, he learned that he doesn't have to carry the world on his shoulders.

If you can identify with this and recognize yourself to be parentally inverted, resign as the general manager of the universe—and know with gleeful chagrin that somehow God manages to get along without your help! You may have to repeat this again and again until your spirit takes this in automatically.

You may find that you got into wrong positions with other siblings, as I did. That usurps and prevents right relationships. Never mind that someone has to do the job; the lateral side of whatever is not done by the right person is damage—or the right thing is done by the wrong person.

Again the antidote is for you to repent and accept forgiveness from God. The blood of Jesus will wash away resentments from your heart if you were a child who experienced this. His perfect love will cast away the hidden fears that have propelled overstriving. The cross will effect death of resultant structures—busyness, self-suffering stances of martyrdom, controlling, putting others down, and so on. Such "practices" (as we see in Colossians 3:9) all may need to be seen and dealt with one by one or may simply die and wither away as deeper taproots are dealt with. The presence of the Father can heal and restore your tired and untrusting heart.

Substitute Spouse

A second more confusing and damaging condition may follow upon parental inversion. You may have grown up in a home where one of your parents failed because of physical or mental health or addiction. Or you may be one whose parent left the home or who died when you were younger. You may have taken steps to fill the vacant spot. In most homes like this, it is either the oldest or the most sensitive (and thus giving) child of the opposite sex as the remaining or still functioning parent. As a boy or young man, you may have become the breadwinner or your mother's confidant or her strength to lean upon. As a girl, you may have awakened early to prepare your father's clothes and lunch for work. You may have been the one to discipline your younger siblings. In short, in one degree or another, you may have set about to run the household in your father's or mother's place. That put you in position as a spouse—without the bed. An undercurrent of nuances of meaning and practiced mate feelings flows between you and your parent, though unwanted and uninvited. The stance invokes them.

Even if your mother never let herself think a sexual thought toward you as her son, you were in position, and stimuli flow, purely from being in that position. If you never thought a sexual thought toward your mother, you still unconsciously turned off untoward feelings and stimuli. Somewhere deep in your subconscious, the thought is, "This is my mother; I must not think or feel that way." Or you may have had conscious feelings and consciously refused them. The result is that a pattern of withdrawal and shutting down is built into the passages of your heart.

Now, you may be the model husband, trained to be responsible, knowing how to be strength for your wife. But what can happen to many who were raised in a home like what was described above is that suddenly and unaccountably they may be unable to make love to their wives. There is no impotency, but they are merely turned off. Something is blocking them, and they can't imagine what. The block is a built-in turn-off mechanism activated usually the moment the wife becomes a mother. The turn-off mechanism is then activated by projection-identification processes.

One young man came to me completely frustrated and bewildered. He loved his beautiful wife, and he had greatly enjoyed and found fulfillment in sexual intercourse. Now he couldn't bring himself to touch her. He kept thinking something about "respecting her too much," but that didn't square at all either with his ideas about sex or his previous freedom to enjoy her body. It turned out that his lovely mother had been divorced just as he entered puberty, and he had tried to be strong and protective for her. Her beauty had affected him. He could remember, as we talked, having to turn off his feelings. We simply forgave the boy his confused feelings and commanded that old, no-longer-needed turn-off structure to loose its hold on him and set him free from identifying his wife and mother as one. His wife wrote (with him) in great happiness, thanking me for returning her husband to her. The blockage has never returned. Praise the Lord.

The same may happen the other way around. You may be a daughter whose mother died, became an invalid, or simply failed. You may have stepped in to clean the house, shop, cook, do the laundry, and whatever else may have been necessary, including watching over younger siblings. You were put in position as a mate, with the same confused, unconscious feelings and results.

However, there are instances where there is no such crossover between the sexes, simply that a daughter takes over in the father's place to help her mother, or a son in the mother's place to help the father. Confusions still abound, for each is acting in a position not natural for them as children or teenagers. The girl may become too manly or at least so learn to try to run the home that she has difficulty later letting her husband be head of the home. Or a boy may learn wifely roles and unconsciously seek them until that becomes confusing and seductive to his wife, inducing her to play the vacant authority role.

However, far more damaging and more common than caring for parents physically is caring for them emotionally. If your parents were weak or broken, they may have used you as a salve for their own pain, as a comforter and confidant. That may have seemed good, and the parents may have been unaware any damage could result. They may have used a number of manipulative tactics to get you to fill the empty place their own parents left empty. For instance, they may have held you in order to be held. They may have used guilt to coerce your love and gratitude. They may have said things such as, "After all I do for you, and this is the thanks I get?" They may have put themselves down to coax you to compliment them. They may have expected you to simply know what they needed without having to ask, becoming distraught when you didn't know. They may have played the martyr, saying, "You go on and have a good time. I'll just sit here at home all by myself."

Rather than impart identity, your parents may have swallowed up your identity into their own. They may have done what you should have done for yourself, and then acted hurt at the first sign of protest. Not having their own clear sense of self, they may have required you to affirm them by echoing all of their personal tastes and opinions, and felt betrayed by any like, dislike, or opinion different from their own.

Parental inversion distorts discipline. Inverted parents may take misbehavior as a personal affront, overreacting indignantly, saying things like, "How could you do this to me?" They may punish through pouting or acting hurt, demanding comfort, yet refusing it. Or they may use the silent treatment, turning punishment into banishment.

Even in your parents' attempts to comfort you, it was often more about them than it was about you. They may have felt so overwrought over your woes that you had to stuff down all of your hurt to comfort them.

Even if your parents never employed any of these tactics, you may have been a sensitive, burden-bearing child who still became parentally inverted by sensing your parents' pain and coming to the rescue. One girl's parents applauded her stage performance, but she could sense that they were secretly embarrassed at her mistakes. So she "protected" them from any further embarrassment by squelching any future attempts to be creative!

The effect of all this is that childhood is stolen. You didn't get to be a child. At all costs, you had to be strong to keep the adult world from imploding. To keep up the strong façade, you may have suppressed a cauldron of hurt, resentment, and anger about being used to gratify adults. You could not allow others to know about the whirlwind of confusions at having to sort out your parents' crazy-making messages, nor could you let yourself know. You could not allow yourself to need, only to give. When you were allowed (or required) to receive, it was to make your parents feel good about giving. The message was, "Show me by your response that I am a good parent." In short, you were required to provide your parents with self-esteem.

We now want to lay the groundwork for healing, but there is a cost you must pay. You must admit that your childhood world was in chaos and that you truly did not hold it together as you may have thought. You must admit the fact that you were and are still confused, and that you need to learn to be able to distinguish where others end and you begin. Still more difficult is the realization that you were (and are still) filled with suppressed emotions that you had always regarded as weak. You may find that you need help as all these things unravel. The validation from a mature

Christian friend or prayer minister who is open and transparent would be beneficial to you. Persevere through the healing process until you are able to feel what you really feel and think what you truly think, without shame or fear that the world will fly apart if you dare to take the time out to be yourself.

HEALING FOR YOUR PAST

You may have had any one or even a combination of these things occur in your upbringing, but once seen, these issues are easily prayed about. Ask God to help you break out of the old mold and find and build into you a new identity in Christ. Don't try to build a new self, but discover and celebrate the new identity resurrecting out of the old. Appreciate and praise God for what He is doing in making you new, thus healing the first and deepest hurt—lack of ability to trust the Father.

The concepts of parental inversion and substitute mate are simple. You can see easily how such patterns are formed in the heart. It may not be so easy to overcome them, once fully installed, but you must take a firm hold on your own healing.

Taking over responsibility for your parent is not an easy thing to hate as sin. The difficulty is that it has become a most noble definition of life. The whole purpose of life may be invested in it, justified a thousand times scripturally. How about, "Greater love has no one than this, that one lay down his life for his friends" (John 15:13)? Another scripture that may be used is:

> Then the righteous will answer Him, saying, "Lord, when did we see You hungry, and feed You, or thirsty, and give You drink? And when did we see You a stranger, and invite You in, or naked, and clothe You? And when did we see You sick, or

in prison, and come to You?" And the King will answer and say to them, "Truly I say to you, to the extent that you did it to one of these brothers of Mine, even the least of them, you did it to Me."

—Matthew 25:37–40

Who were more deserving "brothers" than our own parents? Our entire life has been a commitment to serve. How hard it may be to see that as sin. Let us be as clear then as possible. Our serving was not wrong. It never has been. God wants to reward us for it. But our motive for serving was not pure. That impurity made some of our serving as much or more damaging than helpful. It is for that wrong motivation that the Lord calls us to death. It is a good death; we will most likely never stop serving. God loves us for it: "You are My friends, if you do what I command you" (John 15:14). "Jesus answered and said to him, 'If anyone loves Me, he will keep My word; and My Father will love him, and We will come to him, and make Our abode with him'" (John 14:23). Our death will mean that corruptions of the flesh will die and fade away from our serving (1 Pet. 1:24). Striving will die, and it will become the Holy Spirit who prompts and checks what we do, not the compulsions of flesh.

PI and substitute mate are not simply attitudes; they are habit structures. Prayer may initiate struggle, not end it. You will be called upon again and again by family, friends, or co-workers to check habitual thoughtless responses that you may have that revert back to old ways. Here we plead with you to develop humility. God will allow someone to whom you are accountable to point out facets of your behavior that are motivated through PI. The Holy Spirit will teach, rebuke, correct, and counsel you through the body. You must be willing to hear the frequent admonitions and rebukes of friends. "Speaking the truth in love, we are to grow up in all aspects into Him, who is the head, even Christ" (Eph. 4:15). No one likes to hear rebuke, but Scripture is clear about it. "Stern discipline is for him who forsakes the way; he who hates reproof will die" (Prov. 15:10). "He is on the path of life who heeds instruction, but he who forsakes reproof goes astray" (Prov. 10:17). "Whoever loves discipline loves knowledge, but he who hates reproof is stupid" (Prov. 12:1). "Poverty and shame will come to him who neglects discipline, but he who regards reproof will be honored" (Prov. 13:18).

When I (John) was a child, swollen adenoids and tonsils created a habit of breathing through my mouth. When I was seven, a tonsillectomy enabled me to breathe through my nose, but the habit of breathing through my mouth had long been established. My father instructed all the family to keep saying to me constantly, "Shut your mouth, Jackie." And he ordered me never to be mad at them but to appreciate it as love and take it. They did, day after day, and finally the habit was broken. More importantly, their continual corrections built into me an appreciation for brothers' reproofs as love, well meant for me, and an ability to take it. For that reason the Lord has blessed me with brothers who do chastise me regularly. They may not always feel that their words did much good, but I have never been angry or hated them for the words. That childhood experience taught me to love correction and those who do it. "Do not reprove a scoffer, lest he hate you, reprove a wise man, and he will love you" (Prov. 9:8). That capacity is vital for those of us who are afflicted with PI. If brothers and sisters can't feel free to let us know when we are trampling all over them or doing too much, they are not likely to speak the truth often enough to us; so we are not likely to break the habit. It is difficult enough to rebuke someone who is obviously doing wrong; it is much more difficult to correct someone who is trying to be helpful. Truly, "Faithful are the wounds of a friend, but deceitful are the kisses of an enemy" (Prov. 27:6).

In short, PI and substitute mate are practices in the flesh (Col. 3:9) but about which the Lord has far more compassion than we do. To be corrected is to be rewarded. God has chosen to set us free. He wants to bless us. Freedom means, then, that the Holy Spirit will serve through us restfully, even if perhaps more actively than before, but He will observe the checkpoints and give us wisdom to serve in ways that bless.

CHAPTER 3

FINDING IDENTITY AND CALLING

My child, when you come to serve the Lord, prepare yourself for testing. Set your heart right and be steadfast, and do not be impetuous in time of calamity. Cling to him and do not depart, so that your last days may be prosperous. Accept whatever befalls you, and in times of humiliation be patient. For gold is tested in the fire, and those found acceptable, in the furnace of humiliation. Trust in him, and he will help you; make your ways straight, and hope in him.

—SIRACH 2:1–6, NRSV, THE APOCRYPHA

There is an appointed time for everything. And there is a time for every event under heaven—a time to give birth, and a time to die; a time to plant, and a time to uproot what is planted. A time to kill, and a time to heal; a time to tear down, and a time to build up. A time to weep, and a time to laugh; a time to mourn, and a time to dance. A time to throw stones, and a time to gather stones; a time to embrace, and a time to shun embracing. A time to search, and a time to give up as lost; a time to keep, and a time to throw away. A time to tear apart, and a time to sew together; a time to be silent, and a time to speak. A time to love, and a time to hate; a time for war, and a time for peace.

—ECCLESIASTES 3:1–8

There are two great and conflicting lessons to be learned in maturation. One is called individuation, which means separating yourself from all formative influences and becoming your own person. The other is incorporation— to become a corporate person, part of a group, sensitive to the desires and wishes of others. One definition of maturity is to learn to think in "we" terms rather than only "me, myself, and I." These two tasks cross over in conflict drastically—and both are tasks that we deal with during our teen years.

As a teenager it may have been difficult to find the balance between being free to be your own person and yet being part of your family. From ages thirteen to fifteen, Mom and Dad may have treated you as though you were still ten and expected you to step to old family loyalties and activities when other drummers beat wildly in your ears. At eighteen, college cliques clamored for conformity just when your bones cried out for individuality. About nineteen to twenty-one, no sooner than you became your own person did genes and juices start working trying to unite you to a spouse—and corporateness.

This process of alternation between individuating and incorpo-rating is very important, because without individuation, we cannot become healthily corporate. We either cop out from who we are to mimic accepted group roles and dynamics, or we try to beat the drum everyone else must step to. Only when you are a fully free individual will you have what is needed to give yourself to a group and to accept the give and take of healthy relationships.

Let us now follow this process from individuation and internalization to incorporation.

THE TASK OF BECOMING CORPORATE

A teenager has two primary tasks before becoming corporate. First, he must individuate, or cut free from everything and everyone who has formed him—who has birthed, fed, housed, clothed, instructed, disciplined, and given him love. Second, he must internalize. Everything in his life has come to him from outside him, from others. None of it has yet become fully his own, from within. Since he may "own" many possessions and the family is his, his parents may say, "Everything we have is yours," not comprehending how he feels, since it was all theirs given to him, not something of his own creation and choosing as a mature person from within himself. He must now ponder all the teaching and examples of his parents (and teachers), burn his fingers, and find out for himself why law is law and life is what it is. Wisdom, understanding, morality and faith, purpose and ambition, habits and practices, fellowship and joys, all must become his own by the painful process of inner wrestling with his own thoughts and emotions. There is no shortcut, no easy way to do it. Individuation and internalization are the Scylla and Charybdis* through which he must pass or fail to become an adult.

---

*An idiom expressing great opposing difficulties, from early navigational problems; Scylla—a promontory difficult to pass (off southern Italy); Charybdis—a whirlpool opposite the entrance to Messina, also in southern Italy

Individuation

Individuation does not begin with the teenage years; it climaxes there. It begins at the moment of formation in the womb, as cells become their own entity, not the mother. Were the cells to be absorbed, no new life could begin. Individuation is the price of life. Birth means further individuation. Cutting the umbilical cord forces becoming organically one's own entity. Weaning, managing to walk rather than be carried, learning to talk, mastering the toilet—all are steps effecting individuation. Failure to accomplish any of these reduces the person to dependence and so reconnects the umbilical cord emotionally.

Individuation is accomplished first externally and then internally; first physically, then mentally; and finally, emotionally and morally, then spiritually. Birth and weaning begin to break organic dependence. Each lesson cuts more physical dependencies— walking, handling one's own table utensils, dressing oneself, and so on. However, long beyond infancy we remain not only physically but also emotionally and mentally dependent. Going to school initiates the process of mental weaning and the beginnings of emotional individuation. But these are only begun. Morality and spirituality are still nascent, formative, and dependent. Each step—Sunday school, public school, exams and discipleship, church attendance, interaction with friends, and so on—calls for further and more interior individuation.

During the teenage years it climaxes like a volcano, long bubbling to eruption. What makes the trouble usually is a two-sided squeeze. On the one hand, the father and mother may be unprepared to handle a teenager or even to admit their son or daughter is that old. They may not realize what is happening inside him, seeing all his changes in behavior as something horrible, something needing to be corrected by tightening down the screws. On the other hand, most teenagers cannot be consistent. One moment a young person may be responsible and sensitive, and the next he becomes totally self-centered and irresponsible. One moment he wants to brave the world, and in the next, he has fled halfway back to the womb. Normally, without training, neither parents nor teenagers understand or even are conscious of what is going on. Subliminal forces push, and old patterns no longer can contain the new urges. Impulses may be tried and rebuffed or not tried and repressed. Attempts at communication batten down doors to empty rooms— neither the parent nor the teenager occupy those places anymore, and neither realizes it.

Teenage individuation becomes more difficult by the fact that the very loved ones who have given everything a teenager is have now become the problem! Even if parents are wise enough to understand and let their teenager try some things, they—their love, their presence, their thinking—are now in the way of finding one's own—the second task, internalization. We must stand against the very people we want to love and admire, and more cogently whose approval we need, at the very moment when, if they give it, we seem sometimes to be put down to childhood again, or the enterprise of discovery has been stolen from us.

Surely the prodigal son of Luke 15 was the sinner we have all heard sermons about, but one thing needs to be said in his favor. Though asking for his share of his family's good was tantamount to wishing his father were already dead, he was at least doing what every teenager must do—taking hold of what is his own in order to individuate and internalize. The cost was all his substance (perhaps he could have learned an easier way), but it was not merely an expression of largesse that when he returned his father placed the ring of authority on his finger and the robe of ruling on his shoulders (Luke 15:22). His father saw that he had become his own man. He was now qualified to rule. We can now easily see that the remark of the elder brother is that of an unindividuated child:

> But he answered and said to his father, "Look! For so many years I have been serving you, and I have never neglected a command of yours; and yet you have never given me a kid, that I might be merry with my friends; but when this son of yours came, who has devoured your wealth with harlots, you killed the fattened calf for him."
>
> —LUKE 15:29–30

Internalization

Internalization means that as much as a teenager may admire his parents and desire to keep their moral ways, he must not simply do so or he fails to become his own person. He must examine morality for himself, testing and seeing. He must now work through what his parents may have long forgotten they also had to examine and think their way through. But it is not merely a mental process. It is as though each ethical and moral law has to be felt through with deep, inner, and unseen fingers of his spirit, testing to see whether he really wants to own these things as his own. If he could see clearly and get at it, the task would be easy. But he cannot. It is necessarily a "fumble through" process. Incidents have to happen that reveal to him, often by pain of loss, where his heart really stands.

Being a late bloomer, I was still working through some things as late as twenty-three when I was in seminary. I remember wrestling with the fact that I had thought through everything so mentally and therefore had remained so much in control that I was not certain whether my philosophy of life actually fit where my heart was or not. I felt as though all my thinking were somewhat like a flying carpet, maybe not settled down on reality at all, maybe askew of where life really is. At the time, I was working at Delta C and S Airlines, Midway Airport, Chicago, as the night shift foreman in charge of unloading and loading all aircraft on my shift. I managed to organize the crews to maximum efficiency but kept thinking that I needed something to happen totally out of my control so I could see by my reactions where my heart really was.

Then a lazy, inefficient, loud-mouthed Archie Bunker–type was placed in my command. No matter what orders were given, or how kindly, he spat back obscenities and failed to do his job. The boss would not fire him. His hateful, slothful ways disrupted both crews. One night he bungled so badly that I spoke sharply. He swung at me and missed, but he knocked off my glasses. Still under control, I told him calmly that if they were broken (a crew member was chasing after them in the wind of the prop wash), I would make him pay. I meant I would report it and the cost would have to be deducted from his wages (the common practice in those days). He took it as a challenge to fight and swung a fist at me on the ramp, in public, while passengers were deplaning—a place where I never would have chosen to fight.

That blew my control. I went out of my head with pent-up fury. Though he weighed 250 pounds, I was then a weight lifter, so I ducked under his blows, grabbed him around the waist, picked him up, and smashed him to the pavement. Sitting astraddle him, I grabbed both his wrists with my left hand, holding him immobile, and screamed that I would smash his face with my clenched fist. But then, rising from a deep well, there came into my mind a torrent of Scripture passages and a feeling of compassion. So I did what was actually worse—I chucked him gently under the chin and called him a baby!

That experience locked my thinking into my heart. It began to tell me a part of my reality. I could hate. I could want to kill. I could be worse than cruel. I could lose control. But another part of me, deeper it seemed, chose kindness and tried to hold me to it, while another part turned it again to cruelty. From all that, I could see that my choosing of the Lord's Word was not something exterior. In a moment of crisis the Word had flooded my mind as something I had chosen from deep within.

You may have had many such experiences—a fender bender (of your dad's brand-new car), too much sexual exploration, an escapade with some street gang on the shady side of the law, and so on. Left alone or met with compassion and trust, you can use such experiences as the gristmill for grinding all your thoughts and emotions into the powder of repentance and change. You can discover your own reality and commence to stand up to life as an adult.

You can probably recall what happened when your parents heard of some misdoing. They may have come down like avenging angels, determined to straighten you out. Or maybe you are a parent of a teenager who has done something like this. Parents must be careful. In circumstances such as these, a teenager can be robbed of the enterprise of discovery, forcing him to defend the very thing he would have used to discover reality and return to sensibility. Unfortunately, then, he must reach further into degradation to find some area not already preempted by his parents in order to find himself. Repeated altercations may cause him, by rebellion, to become stuck in the mire of ways he would not have owned at all were his parents (or others) not riding him so hard.

It requires courage to individuate and internalize. Those who have strength of spirit (Eph. 3:16) can do it, and those who do not cannot. We must individuate at the time our inner being calls for it, each person within his own timetable, or we do so later at great peril or not at all. Too many times young women have come to us having moved too quickly from their father's house to submission to a husband, not having internalized and individuated. Now, urges are upon them that are blocked by wifely and parental duties. Such women cannot conveniently find the space and time to accomplish what should have been done earlier.

Incorporation and individuation are interwoven tasks that alternate in predominance and importance throughout life. Each step must be accomplished in its proper time, and the next individuation or incorporation cannot be entered unless the previous is successfully completed. Immediately after birth, the first necessity is to learn to be corporate. A child's first stage of development is absorbed in learning basic trust, the basic building block that enables corporate life in adulthood. A baby must learn to open his spirit, to flow into others and receive others to himself. He must learn capacity to hold open to others despite woundings.

Basic trust, as the first building block of corporateness, is also the absolute prerequisite for the next step—individuation—saying no. If a child at two has not accomplished the corporate task of basic trust, he cannot master the next task of individuation. It takes courage for a two-year-old to say no to those adults who supply everything he must have to survive. His saying no is a practice in the art of individuating, of saying, "I am not you, and you are not me. I am my own person."

Since he has failed to incorporate (to build basic trust) and therefore cannot successfully individuate (by saying no), he cannot graduate to the next lesson of incorporation, to play with instead of alongside of others. He must then either dominate and control or go along meekly with whatever his friends decide to do. He cannot say a proper yes or no to them; he either controls or is controlled.

When Ecclesiastes 3 says there is a time for all things (quoted at the beginning of this chapter), that is not merely a philosophical exercise affecting nothing other than the fun of thinking about things. That is also a description of a principle in the maturation process of human beings—indeed, of all living things. The principle is that there is a time ordained by the Lord's wisdom for all things to develop in sequential order. Whatever does not accomplish its task in its season is out of order—and in trouble! Perhaps for this reason Jesus cursed the fig tree (Matt. 21:19; Mark 11:14). It had made all the appearances of producing fruit early, out of season, but it had no fruit. It was a sick plant, off kilter, out of time and harmony, producing nothing.

A child who fails to learn basic trust in his first mental year must struggle later, out of time and place, to achieve what should have been learned earlier. What schoolteacher has not pitied and struggled to help immature children who at seven or eight have not attained the social skills appropriate for children who are two, three, four, and five? The principle is stern and unrelenting: whatever is not learned easily in the right time and sequence will have to be fulfilled, with difficulty, in the wrong order and sequence. A man who has not individuated from his mother cannot incorporate with his wife until he does cut free later, usually with much struggle. A woman who has not been wholesomely corporate with her father in earliest life cannot fully individuate from him in teenage years and cannot later become wholly corporate with her husband—but she must learn to do so, out of time and sequence, the hard way.

In our own lives the Holy Spirit can train us to be like detectives to notice what is out of time and place. He will help us to see what doesn't fit. Our Lord will help us comprehend the planned sequence of God for maturation. Through His leading we can sense the jarring presence of what is out of place and start looking for it. Astronomers discovered some of our planets by puzzling over the irregularities—the jarring aspect—in the orbits of other planets, until they saw by inference that something had to be creating the disorder and hunted until the unseen planet was discovered. Just so, the Holy Spirit will guide us to understand the true orbits of maturation so we can sense that by something being out of place or out of order in time and sequence, some sinful condition must have been blocking maturation somewhere in the past (and is still doing so), needing only to be discovered and repented of to become light (Eph. 5:13).

A man came whose wife was leaving him. His was a nationally known media ministry, and she was a minister's daughter who had moved early from her father's strict home to her husband's exposed righteous style of life. Now at thirty plus, she wanted to do all the things she had been denied during her teenage years. She thought she wanted to smoke and drink, date and dance. Her husband, his work, and her children had become identified as the prison of her life. Friends saw her as plagued by demons of lust and prayed accordingly. But lust was only minimally a factor. Internalization and individuation were now clamoring at a woman more than thirty years old to do what should have been done at fifteen to twenty—not that she should have smoked and drank, but that she should have individuated and become her own person. Now she falsely identified becoming herself as a life of carousing.

The prayers of the faithful totally missed her. Her church friends wanted to clamp her into the same behavior she needed to react against and test. Advisors scolded and called upon her "good nature" or her "love of the Lord," whatever handle they could think to get hold of, not realizing they were isolating themselves from her by lining up with the father and the "establishment" against which she needed to test herself. Being thoroughly performance oriented, she could find no acceptable way for acting out her inquiries. For her it was all or nothing—either all the way with Jesus and morality, or all the way into the dregs of sin. Those were not the real options at all! Not understanding her own inner dynamics, she could not comprehend what actually was pushing her. She could only see that those people who smoked and drank and danced were not the ogres she thought she had been taught they were. If that were wrong, perhaps the whole of Christianity was only a performance game. Certainly she could now begin to see the masks and roles people all around her were playing. She finally concluded she wanted out altogether.

Unfortunately, none in the body around her comprehended what she was actually proceeding through. They only wanted to chase demons or scold her to return to acceptable roles. Her need to throw it all over was actually only a need to cut free, thrown into oversized rebellion by the trap of performance orientation. Had she been helped to understand, she could have been allowed to test and try things, suffered to do so by a wise and supportive body and husband. Finally she wound up divorcing her husband and throwing herself with abandon into rank sin.

I (John) was called in—too late, of course. She could only view my attempt as another clever ploy to pull her back into the fold, no matter what I said or didn't say or do. In fact, since she had children, what else at the outset could I do for her? I could not set her free to abandon her responsibilities to her children, much as I knew she needed that freedom. Praise God that she had gained the courage to try to become her own person, but what a tragedy that it came so late!

Presently there is an epidemic across the country of dutiful mothers suddenly throwing off the traces and opting for the wild life. Some fathers also are abandoning their families. Among the many causes, often foremost is the lack of teenage individuation and thus also failure to incorporate. A wedding had happened; real marriage had not followed.

I can think of three ministers' daughters to whom I have ministered, all three having received some counsel, too late, from me. All three left their husbands, sampled the wild life, and are now divorced. We were not given opportunity soon enough to save them or their marriages. All three were regarded by relatives, friends, and their churches as having been seduced by lust.

The Church must be trained to minister wisely and quickly to those who are working through this process late in life. There is healing and restoration in the body of Christ through God's power. Late individuation cannot and ought not be prevented or healed, but we who have been given the grace to walk through this during the right time and season must stand by ready to pick up the pieces, comprehending with compassion and mercy. Our Lord came to set people free to become mature. Perhaps this is one application of the cryptic words of Jesus in Matthew 10:34–35:

Do not think that I came to bring peace on the earth; I did not come to bring peace, but a sword. For I came to set a man against his father, and a daughter against her mother, and a daughter-in-law against her mother-in-law.

Observe again the clarity of God's Word:

But as many as received Him, to them He gave the right to become children of God, even to those who believe in His name.

—JOHN 1:12

This verse above does not say that those who received Him automatically and instantly became children of God. Of course in one sense we do. But St. John means something more than that. He says, "...the right to become." That speaks of a process—the process of maturing into Christ as sons and daughters.

How carefully can we say and our readers receive what follows? Can Jesus's comparison of the prodigal son with the elder son say, among other things, that He views maturation in Christ as more valuable than always being good? Suppose we have two children, the first being one who has stumbled a number of times and returned eventually through it all to become wise and free, and the second one who has always been a model of good behavior, but with whom we cannot have the fullness of heartfelt laughter and banter because he is not real. He is always performing to please us. Which son are we more relaxed around? Which one has indeed become a son? The performing one remains a servant, trying to please us. The stumbling one has become a son with whom we can have a depth of fellowship the performer knows nothing about.

Are we advocating sin? Far be it from us. Many can individuate and internalize without falling into rebellion and immorality.

But we are saying that if we cannot individuate any other way, I am sure the Lord would rather we rebel and so become our own rather than remain as a performing Pharisee! I believe our Lord paid the price on the cross for us to become sons, not servants only. We write this hopefully as a death knell to the scolders and a word of hope and faith to those whose sons are still rebelling. What such sons are doing is not all bad, and parents did something right or the child would not have had the courage to try something.

Our word to you, parents, is this: let them go. The sooner they are released, the less each must rebel. We do not mean permissiveness. Rules must remain. We speak of inner letting go expressed outwardly as compassion and understanding.

What those who individuate need is trust—not naïveté that really expects them to conform to good behavior and that says, "I trust you to be good." But they need the kind of trust that says, "I know you are going to make mistakes. I know you have to find things out. I trust what is in God and in you to come through it. I let you go, but I stand beside you in love."

Consider this: our loving Father knew, before any of us were born, just how badly we would sin and mess up our lives and the lives of those around us. But He did not withhold us from life. He set us free to make our mistakes, and He paid the price for our freedom and maturation through His Son's death for us. Was He a bad Father because He let us go and gave us freedom though He could have forced us to be good? Every parent must pay the same price in setting children free.

If our parents have not trained moral values into us before our teenage years, it is too late. The time for training was from birth to age twelve. Some training can continue, of course, but these become only embellishments. Foundation stones must be laid at the right time, in childhood, not later.

Some may question statements that things must be learned at times ordained by God, but this principle applies throughout nature. A seed of a tree must first open in the earth, then send its roots down, before reaching for sunlight and growth above ground. Life cannot come any other way. How impossible if a seed were to try to produce leaves and fruit while still underground! Akin to plants, we are designed to develop in physical growth and social skills in divinely planned order. When we are prevented or fail of our own volition, trouble ensues.

Our attempt is to teach you how to handle this process of individuation, one, as a parent of teenagers, two, as one who may be going through this process as an adult, and three, as the spouse of someone who had not been given the chance to walk through this as a young person.

To the Parents of Teenagers

Christian parents sometimes fail with teenagers more miserably than unbelievers, precisely because they try too hard. Teenagers of nonbelievers, who may not keep such strict watch, may be freer to try things and sooner find out which things are unprofitable (if they had some basic training and affection—otherwise they just become even more thoroughly lost). Unfortunately, whereas in former years a teenager might have only run the legs off his dad's best stallion, today he can fry his brains with drugs, smash his body beyond repair in an instant in a speeding car, and find ways to explore sex far beyond the opportunities of earlier generations. Fear thus prompts dutiful parents to tighten the screws of control, and so all too frequently teenagers are propelled into becoming trapped in things they would only have tasted if left to their own wisdom.

The key factor is the cross. Can parents pay the price of self-death, pain, and fear and pray faithfully until the teenager finds himself?

If love, affection, discipline, and understanding were present in a teenager's childhood, if quality and quantity of experiences were shared, a teenager has what it takes to burn his fingers lightly and return to society wiser and freer. But if there has been little physical touch, little talk and understanding, and few compliments and affirmations, residual hidden angers are almost sure to tempt him to turn normal cutting free into rebellion and immorality.

Sometimes it is good to get help from someone who is trained and called to deal with teenagers at this stage, such as a prayer minister or youth pastor. In the body, we need not feel as parents that there isn't help or hope for us and our children as we try and fail to move into complete, functional parts of the whole. Teenagers will seldom seek counsel and help on their own. Most often they arrive in the office of their youth pastor or prayer minister sullenly, feeling coerced and trapped, expecting to be worked on and manipulated to return to harness. They are prepared to resist anything but open honesty and trust. Ordinarily they are also frightened about themselves and wish they could talk about it, but they steel themselves not to for fear of being cajoled by sympathy into returning to mental chains.

Our word: get *with*, not over against. Prayer ministers or youth pastors must get out of the trap of being the parents' representative to work *on* the teenagers. I (John) usually begin by asking, "Tom, are you here today because you want to be, or do you feel trapped?" We talk awhile about that. I don't try to convince him I am not an extension of his parents' controlling arm. That position of trust has to be won, not sold. He would feel "soaped" otherwise.

There is a principle in Scripture that is a guideline for ministry to teenagers (or anyone else): "Weep with those who weep" (Rom. 12:15). Teenagers in rebellion and in need of ministry are weeping inwardly, though most would not want to admit it. They weep and ache within their hearts because their parents fail to understand them. They hurt about themselves and may need to be angry with someone else, anyone else, because they find themselves acting in ways they actually despise while outwardly claiming how much fun they are having. So I weep with them. I say, "I'd like to share something with you if you don't mind." I share briefly about individuation and internalization and then say, "The trouble is most parents don't understand that. They don't know how to let go. They treat a young man like he's eight or ten and then can't understand why he gets mad. They don't trust you to use your own good common sense. And they order you to do something as though you wouldn't have thought of it yourself, and it makes you mad as though you were a little kid or something."

After a little such sharing, a teenager will usually blurt out something like, "Yeah, well, how come she won't ever get off my case? What's wrong with coming in a little late . . . or wearing my hair like I want . . . or running around with so-and-so?" He (or she) is beginning to trust and open up. I don't try to defend the parents' position or explain his parents to a teenager. It's still time to commiserate, so it's, "Yeah, they can't stand that, can they?" Or, "You wonder why it's such a big deal." That may open the floodgates to a long session of griping and sharing. Prayer ministers must bite their tongues not to step in to correct, advise, explain, or defend; they only need to listen. Prayer ministers may feel like traitors to the parents and wonder whether they are helping a teenager to excuse himself when he ought to be hauled to account. But when trust is fully established and "catharting" (getting it all out) has been allowed, real back-and-forth talk can begin, not before.

We do not usually enter immediately into deep inner healing with teenagers. We will, if some particularly bothersome character trait needs attention, quite apart from the problem of teenage development itself. A wise maxim is this: if everything is being torn up on the inside, keep everything in place on the outside. That is, if inner trauma is going on, keep the job, friends, church, and all other associations unchanged if possible. Inversely, if job, home, church, and other relationships are all being changed, don't tackle inner problems until things settle down. If the outer world is in flux, don't stir the inner. Don't fight both worlds at once—if you can help it. A teenager's associations are all in flux, and his inner world is already being torn up by individuation and internalization, so it is not a wise time to try to do much inner healing.

The first thing a prayer minister will want to do with a teenager is to establish a base away from home. He will want to be someone who will come alongside him, who isn't going to treat him like a child, who will hear whatever he has to say, who won't preach at him or immediately try to set him straight. Above all, he will want to be someone who won't take out of the teen's hands the initiative of his life and who won't give him answers he needs to come to himself.

Some teenagers often will try to use what the prayer minister says against their parents, sometimes stretching things and putting words in the prayer minister's mouth. Therefore the prayer minister needs to have sessions with the parents, explaining carefully what their teenager is going through and how the prayer minister must first become a listening post. The prayer minister should tell the parents not to expect great changes overnight and not to worry if it appears as if he is supporting their son or daughter in wrong ways of thinking. Having grown up in ranch country, I sometimes say, "You know, down on the ranch we discovered the best way to turn a stampede of wild horses was to run with them awhile. Then we could begin to turn the leaders. I'll have to do that with your son/daughter until he/she can hear what I have to say without being turned off. You know my stand for the Lord and for good morals. Bear with us awhile."

Sometimes such a dynamic is engaged between a young person and one or both parents that they can't stop. Mama (usually rather than Papa in most Western cultures) may not be able to stop her tongue. She persists in scolding and correcting, and the teenager keeps on reacting. In such cases we have no hesitation to talk with the parents about letting their teenager live for a while with some relative or close friend. A change of environment helps. Usually after enough experimentation and pain, a teenager wants to change, but the demanding tongue of his mother (or his father) prevents his freedom to choose what is right. He finds himself defending what he actually wants to turn away from. In a new environment he doesn't have to swim upstream against a backlog of remembrances and accusations. In a new situation, choosing to make right decisions is no longer equated with copping out from being his own person. Out from under the shadow of his parents, he can choose and act out the very thing they want, only now it's his own and not compliance.

My older brother went to live with my aunt Tresia for a while. Paula's sister spent her last two years of high school with us. Their parents loved them enough to allow that solution to conflict. Later, they became sturdy Christian people holding extremely responsible jobs, and they were free enough to be closely related to their parents.

My older brother had "burned his fingers" in a few sinful escapades. Now, he wanted to turn around and espouse righteousness. But Mama had that ground occupied! If he chose righteousness, he could not be certain it was his own choice rather than copping out and complying with Mama's demands. The moment he moved in with Aunt Tresia, he could turn and be a solid citizen, knowing it was his own choice. It was the same for Paula's sister.

Once a prayer minister has fully established trust and the teenager has settled down somewhat, especially if he has moved into a different home for a while, the prayer minister can begin to minister to deep roots. By then the prayer minister can explain how the Lord can reach to our innermost feelings and how our reactions to what happened in earliest childhood form roots that affect us today. Prayer and counsel then proceed as with any other person. It is amazing how often we have seen young people turn around in their tracks. Young people have grown up in a self-conscious, psychologically oriented society. They can grasp more quickly than most adults what are hidden motives and how those originate. And their characters, like their bones, are not so rigidly set as those of older people. Young people are a delight to minister to, if we can only bite our tongues long enough to earn the position!

TO INDIVIDUATING ADULTS AND THE
SPOUSES WHO LOVE THEM

You may be experiencing tough times, because you may be a person who was a "goody-two-shoes" during teenage years and did not internalize and individuate. Now you are in your twenties, thirties, or forties and beginning at last to try to internalize and individuate. Your spouse and children may feel like a trap and a source of heaviness instead of blessing and fulfillment. It is hard for you to divest yourself of the workload of life that presently defines you, to discover what you would have been and would have wanted if you had not jumped so quickly into harness. Confusion may try to set in as you find it increasingly difficult to discipline yourself to do the menial tasks that seemed fun and even fulfilling before. Depression may set in. Bewildering desires to go out and date may arise.

We have ministered to a number of women whose husbands have actually asked them if they could go out and date occasionally! Usually these men are in the habit of addressing their wives as "Mama," unaware that they have transferred their relationship to their mothers onto their wives. Not having individuated, not having left home (Gen. 2:24), they could not cleave to their wives, and so they related to them as mothers, until hunger for a mate and regression to an adolescent approach to life made them want to date someone other than their wives.

It is worse for women because both maternal instinct and cultural norms more stringently hold them to their roles as wife and mother. To go against these is to be thought the worst of sinners, by one's own self as well. Inner urges cry for freedom, yet they really cry for individuation, but the conscious mind now sees "freedom" as escape from the confinement of roles as the way to find her own person.

Through reading this chapter you begin to understand the past events, and this may help you to comprehend what is presently happening. However, the difficulty is that once entered, the process of individuation is like a runaway freight train—awesomely difficult to brake down to control, perhaps impossible.

For couples, the first step is to understand what is happening; then we suggest these alternative actions:

1. Let your wife or husband have some time and expense money for hobbies, continuing education classes, trips, or whatever relatively safe arena allows for discovery of suppressed talents, skills, and enjoyments.

2. Be careful not to cast your husband or wife in papa or mama roles; say to them and allow them to say occasionally, "Hey, I'm not your mother (or father)."

3. Whatever hobby or program is chosen, grant your husband or wife some space, some area of adventure or discovery that is allowed to be all their own, not too closely tied to you. Ask your spouse enough questions to show interest, but do not appear as an inquisitor of a child.

4. If the wife is a stay-at-home mom, encourage her to find a part-time job or some other enterprise that propels her outside the home enough to feel as though her wings can spread out.

5. Bid yourself to become the teenage date! Don't surrender the field to anyone else. We say, "Get out and kick up your heels together—even if your moral nature means you can only paint the town pink. Have some spontaneous, uninhibited fun somewhere regularly. It's OK to make believe you are teenagers together again. It may not take too many occasions before your spouse feels it's enough—but by then you may enjoy it yourself enough to want to keep at it, and you should. God is better than any earthly parents, and what parents are not happy when their children enjoy life?"

6. Be sensitive to when your spouse wants to be flip- pant and when he or she prefers to be serious. Above all, attempt not to scold or try to haul back to attitudes and emotions the mate is individuating out of.

7. Try to pick up some responsibilities the other person is dropping without being too obtrusive, and espe- cially without complaining, while being sensitive not to allow too much of a cop-out from duty.

All these, and the sixth especially, call for self-denial; there- fore, prayer and the cross are central and essential to success. It's a tough role to play, in which there are no experts, so expect to fumble through. Most importantly, have faith for the other, and trust. Believe that God is able to keep your individuating spouse until he or she finds his or her adult shoes again and wears them more comfortably than before.

When everything is again settled in place in maturity, that may be the time to deal with whatever bitter roots may have surfaced in the process, but not before. Let's not tear up everything at once.

Since it requires strength in our spirits to venture out of familiar roles to find out if we really choose them, we may enter into late individuation immediately after wonderfully blessed times! Maybe you were getting along better than ever, or the Holy Spirit took deeper hold in your heart. Some wonderful happening gave courage to the inner one. Right then, when everything seemed to be the best, is when one or the other may flip out. Prayer ministers can help people to understand that the whole process, whether in teenage years or later in life, is entered not because somebody failed, but because something good has given strength and something good is happening through it all. The call is for patience: "And the seed in the good soil, these are the ones who have heard the word in an honest and good heart, and hold it fast, and bear fruit with perseverance" (Luke 8:15).

DESTINY MALAISE

Once we have individuated and internalized who we are, the next step is to discover and fulfill our destiny. This is the final end of incorporation. We may seek and fulfill an ambition, but that is not the same as accomplishing our destiny. Destiny we see as something more corporate than individual—a contribution to society. Destiny can only come within incorporation because God designed us that way. All references to God's predestination will in the New Testament speak of our place *in the body*:

> Blessed be the God and Father of *our* Lord Jesus Christ, who
> has blessed *us* with every spiritual blessing in the heavenly

places in Christ, just as He chose *us* in Him before the foundation of the world, that *we* should be holy and blameless before Him. In love He predestined *us* to adoption as *sons* through Jesus Christ to Himself, according to the kind intention of His will, to the praise of the glory of His grace, which He freely bestowed on *us* in the Beloved.

—Ephesians 1:3–6, emphasis added

He made known to *us* the mystery of His will, according to His kind intention which He purposed in Him with a view to an administration suitable to the fulness of the times, that is, the summing up of all things in Christ, things in the heavens and things upon the earth. In Him also *we* have obtained an inheritance, having been predestined according to His purpose who works all things after the counsel of His will, to the end that *we* who were the first to hope in Christ should be to the praise of His glory.

—Ephesians 1:9–12, emphasis added

So then *you* [plural] are no longer strangers and aliens, but *you* are *fellow citizens with the saints, and are of God's household*, having been built upon the foundation of the apostles and prophets, Christ Jesus Himself being the corner stone, in whom the *whole building, being fitted together* is growing into a holy temple in the Lord; in whom you also are *being built together into a dwelling* of God in the Spirit.

—Ephesians 2:19–22, emphasis added

See also Ephesians 3:4–10; 4:11–16; Romans 12:1–2 (*you* is plural); 1 Peter 1:3–13 (again *you* is plural); and so on.

Destiny malaise is sickness of heart when a person feels he is missing or has already missed the purpose of his life. It is not the same as male or female menopause. It is not the same as the passage a person goes through when it dawns on him that he is not going to set the world on fire, be president of this or that company or social club, invent the great invention, or write a best-selling novel. It is not the same as settling down to become just another Joe Blow, having a family, or doing a job. It is not the same as despondency or depression that can follow the loss of a job or having a business failure or bankruptcy. It is not the same as the blues upon retiring from work or when all the children leave home. It is that deep misery that accompanies the sense of having failed to find one's place to contribute "live works" for God in society.

"For we are His workmanship, created in Christ Jesus for good works, which God prepared beforehand, that we should walk in them" (Eph. 2:10). We all know, in the depth of our spirits, that we have come into life to fulfill a mission. We know there is something laid out for us to do. We sense that our birth in life was timed and planned for that purpose. We speak of it in common daily parlance when death fails to claim us: "Well, I guess He isn't ready for me yet; I've still got something else to do for Him."

> Therefore leaving the elementary teaching about the Christ, let us press on to maturity, not laying again a foundation of repentance from *dead works* and of faith toward God.
> —HEBREWS 6:1, EMPHASIS ADDED

> How much more will the blood of Christ, who through the eternal Spirit offered Himself without blemish to God, cleanse your conscience from *dead works* to serve the living God?
> —HEBREWS 9:14, EMPHASIS ADDED

Dead works are those that originate in our own fleshly striving and whose end, no matter what we profess, is to fulfill our own ego

LETTING GO OF YOUR PAST

needs or give us personal glory. Any service, however high and holy, may be dead works—evangelizing, teaching, healing, working miracles, making mighty prophecies—even as Jesus said to those who prophesied and cast out demons and did many mighty works, "I never knew you; depart from Me, you who practice lawlessness" (Matt. 7:23). Any service, however low or secular, may be live works—carpentry (how could it not be alive while Jesus was in His father's shop?), plumbing, farming, garbage collecting, and so on—even as Jesus said to those in the kingdom, "To the extent that you did it to one of these brothers of Mine, even to the least of them, you did it to Me" (Matt. 25:40).

Live works are those that the Holy Spirit prompts, moves in, and finishes. Live works give glory to God without our having to try to make them so or our saying so. They do because they are His glory. Live works are those done in the flow of the Holy Spirit in our life, done within His plan and purpose from the ground plan of creation for us (Ps. 139:16; Eph. 2:10). Live works happen on the resurrection side, that is, when death of self on the cross is the prelude and He is free to move and do in us, as us, for us.

Live works, no matter how individually done, are accomplished in concert. They are in tune with others, just as a brilliantly executed violin cadenza is still only a part of a concerto. Live works can only happen in fullness in corporate life because God has designed maturation as corporate life (Eph. 4:11–16).

When I was eighteen, my mother informed me that the Lord had appeared to her in a dream eight months before my birth to announce that she would have a son who would be His servant. That set me (or I set myself) to striving to find out what I was created to do. The hurrier I went, the behinder I got. I found nothing out in a hurry. After many years of searching, I gave up and renounced all my striving. I returned the entire mission and purpose to the altar and simply gave myself to Him for whatever purposes He had, willing to walk blindly (Isa. 42:19), only to see in retrospect what may have been accomplished if that were to be His will. I still don't fully know what He wants, but it surely is fun doing what He brings to hand!

Our advice, if you are suffering from destiny malaise, is this: Give it up. Put it all on the altar. Stop searching and striving. Do what comes to hand. Bloom where you are planted. Moses was more than eighty years old when he was called to deliver Israel. Abraham was seventy-four when he was called to leave his country and his father (Gen. 12), and he was over one hundred years of age when Isaac was born. Hurry won't help. We need to die to our self-striving.

We call this teaching the "Abraham-Isaac principle," which is restated by St. Paul in Philippians 3. Whatever gain we have is to be counted as loss (v. 7). We are to cast whatever are our talents and skills, our goals and purposes on the altar, as Abraham obeyed God and would have sacrificed Isaac (Gen. 22:1–18). That sets us free from the grip of it. Now it no longer has us; the Lord has it and us.

Many great, internationally known ministries are in trouble today because (as we perceive it) their leaders have not yet let go and have not placed their ministries on the altar as their Isaac to be sacrificed. So the ministry, rather than the Lord, has them. Their works are mixed with flesh because they are trying to do something for the Lord instead of letting Him do the work through them. They are, therefore, caught in dying works amidst the very signs of thriving life. Not having fullness of death to their own works, they are thus not fully able to allow the Lord full charge of themselves and their ministry. Destiny malaise may become one result if they do not die to their own striving to serve Him.

LETTING GO OF YOUR PAST

Destiny malaise is recognized by unwarranted fatigue, slumping shoulders, or by the opposite—"hype" and overenthusiasm, too much striving and trumped-up emotionalism. Destiny malaise is recognizable through dreams of loss, futile searching, or failing to catch a desired plane or train or some other frustration dream (though not all such dreams indicate destiny malaise). Destiny malaise is most clearly seen by encroaching defensiveness concerning the ministry and one's own part in it. It becomes evident in increasingly controlling and manipulative tactics, especially in advertising and newsletters. It results in multiplying isolation and in consequent attacks upon others.

Overcoming destiny malaise happens when we are willing from the heart to serve in the body in whatever capacity He places us. It is beginning to be conquered when we become willing to listen to all through whom the Lord would counsel us, especially when that counsel arrives through those persons we would ordinarily reject out of hand. It is being overcome when we can see that whatever brother, however errant he seems to us, is part of the body, and that in the seeming confusion he may be hurling at us, God may have a truth He wants us to hear. "Be devoted to one another in brotherly love; give preference to one another in honor" (Rom. 12:10).

"Truly, truly I say to you, when you were younger, you used to gird yourself, and walk wherever you wished; but when you grow old, you will stretch out your hands, and someone else will gird you, and bring you where you do not wish to go" (John 21:18). Although this verse is not actually about individuation, its wording provides an apt metaphor for the process we must all go through. When we are newly born in Christ, we gird ourselves individually and run about going where we will and doing our own thing. We are like children, centered in our own experiences, however much good we do. But when we mature in Christ, we put forth our hands to minister, and others take hold of us and carry us where we would not. The mark of immaturity is a man who insists, as in the great-sounding but faulty poem "Invictus," that "I am the master of my fate; / I am the captain of my soul."[1]

The mark of maturity is willingness, like Jesus, to forgo use of personal power to escape our destiny among brothers. It is to give oneself unreservedly but not unwisely into the hands of others, trusting God though what they do may not be what we would choose at all—like crucifixion! Since Jesus has already accomplished that, often what we receive is only inner death and outward honor, the latter perhaps harder to take. A man who is suffering destiny malaise is surely one who has insisted on "I did it all my way," as the popular ballad proclaims. A brother pastor whom I loved as a coach and shepherd sat down in a chair among brother pastors for ministry. They prayed with glorious accuracy. But he arose to say, "I cannot accept your ministry, my brothers. I know what is best for me, and I must choose my own course." The course he chose led to losing his place of service and to his own brief mental illness.

Francis of Assisi was riding a donkey. A brother on foot screamed at him in anger for riding while the poor walked.

Francis fell on his knees before the man and thanked him for rebuking him. Francis fulfilled his destiny among men before God.

> How good and pleasant it is
>   when brothers live together in unity!
> It is like precious oil poured on the head,
>   running down on the beard,
> running down on Aaron's beard,
>   down upon the collar of his robes.

It is as if the dew of Hermon
    were falling on Mount Zion.
For there the LORD bestows his blessing,
    even life forevermore.

—PSALM 133:1–3, NIV

CHAPTER 4

BECOMING ONE
MEANS *REALLY*
LEAVING FATHER
AND MOTHER

For this cause a man shall leave his father and his mother, and shall cleave to his wife; and they ["the two," Eph. 5:31] shall become one flesh.

—GENESIS 2:24

Listen, O daughter, give attention and incline your ear; forget your people and your father's house.

—PSALM 45:10

Perhaps the greatest inequity in our Western culture is that young people must decide all three major decisions that will affect all their years—their faith, their spouses, and their vocations—before they have time to obtain sufficient wisdom.

Decisions concerning faith and vocation are not so momentarily crucial. Important as it is for an individual to come to faith while still young (Eccles. 12:1), the Lord can redeem and change us later, even from the worst of cults. Some men have found great benefit that their call to vocation came after years of experience in various jobs or other vocations. But marriage is meant to be irreversible. That choice ought not be changed later. Genes and habits of our culture now promote us to choose a spouse before we leave our twenties. That choice will bless us or afflict us (unless the grace of Christ alters) all our life!

Further, our educational system teaches us the basic mechanics— "readin', writin', and 'rithmatic"—and next to nothing of the skills of interpersonal relationships needed for marriage! We are carefully prepared for vocation in on-the-job apprenticeships and vocational, undergraduate, and graduate schools. (See the introduction for more on this.) Churches and Sunday schools endeavor throughout our lives to prepare us for life with God. But for the greatest blessing in this life, our marriage, and for the most important task of life, to raise children, there are no designated schools. Our families, appointed of God to teach (Prov. 1–7; Eph. 6:4), often fail miserably. We launch our children, "while visions of sugar-plums dance in their heads," into what turns out by ignorance and undealt-with flesh to be a hostile sea filled with hidden mines and submarine shots.

We hope to raise up the body of Christ to do prayer ministry, but can we not also plead for preventive medicine? Could not Americans lobby for laws requiring premarital training before marriage licenses are granted? Could we not pass laws forbidding divorce without many months of marital counseling? Could not our high schools have required courses in parental duties and marital relationships? We know how much we all fear the possibility of installing bad teaching. But there are vast areas of noncontroversial general agreement and sound basic wisdom that could and should be taught. The field is full of traps, and who is to say who is to teach or counsel whom, but surely the field needs a legal champion to begin the work.

FINDING

Often, young people have come to Paula and me asking how to know whether the one in whom they are becoming interested is the one for them. We sometimes wish mankind could return to the pattern of biblical days, when parents chose for their children—although if truth were known, that probably wasn't much better! (At least this way we cannot blame the parents; we've made our own bed.)

Many Christians try to push God, their pastor, and/or their prayer minister to tell them whether their intended is His choice or not. That may seem like a good idea, but we suggest that Christians not try to induce God to make up their minds. Other personal choices and consequent steps in relation to God need to be made before the specific question as to which mate. Settle first the question of your life with God. Receive Him not merely as Savior but as Lord. Give your whole life into His care. That gives our courteous Lord the freedom to move the chess pieces of your life, within your free will, so that He can stumble you across the one He planned for you from the beginning.

Normally God won't let us cop out from the decision-making process by telling us who is the one (although He will often confirm or disconfirm your decision once you have made it). Like the wise

Father He is, He wants us to make our own decisions. We often try to turn listening into divination, to find out the future so as to keep out of trouble. But God won't let us do that.

"The mind of a man plans his way, but the LORD directs his steps" (Prov. 16:9). Though a tiny rudder directs a mighty ship, it can have no effect so long as the ship is not moving. Having given your life to the Lord, decide where you are going to work or go to school and church. Commit your life to action in serving Him. Along the way, He will bring to you your mate. (See Genesis 2:18–22.)

We firmly believe in God's providence. We trust His wisdom to know how to let us remain perfectly free and yet manage to cause us to discover the right one. He can move heaven and earth to cause our prospective spouse to cross our path.

Both men and women need to deal with as many interior sin factors as they can while still unattached so that the Lord's first choice can be theirs rather than someone through whom only to reap the worst. Our best preparation to find a husband or wife is first to cleanse and heal our own hearts and minds. Some, perhaps most, change in us can only happen as life with our marriage partner uncovers our sin structures, but at least we want to uncover enough beforehand so as to attract one who can be a help rather than a destruction in the ensuing process. No wonder the Word warns to "remember also your Creator in the days of your youth, *before the evil days come* and the years draw near when you will say, '*I have no delight in them*'" (Eccles. 12:1, emphasis added).

If the Lord brings the woman to the man (Gen. 2:22) and engineers life so we will meet, how shall we be prepared to recognize? How will we know the right one when he or she appears? There are no guarantees, no surefire rules. It is always a heart-in-the-throat business. But here are some clues:

The first is that such discernment does not usually come by romantic fervor. It also does not normally come by "he turns me on" or "she really excites me." We do believe that sometimes there is "love at first sight," but passion is seldom the mark of it. Often it is like a deep recognition in our spirit. Something clicks. A woman often feels an alertness in her spirit and may be surprised at sudden fervor arising in her for his welfare. Seldom do we recognize what it is for quite a while. Paula and I had gone together for almost six months when family financial reverses caused me one spring day to announce that most likely I would not be able to return to college the next fall. Paula knew by the sudden desolation in her heart that I must be the one.

So our second clue is not by good feelings but by hurt. We discover we ache at deeper levels than unfulfilled romantic desire when we are not able to be with the other. Pain strikes when we think that we may not be the ones to raise children, or protect, or bless, or fulfill their days. We may recognize the depth of commitment by fights and flights. The closer we come to realizing what the other means to us, the more we may pick a fight, get wounded, find faults, or do anything to justify fleeing.

One of the most certain signs is that we cease to think about what we want to get from the other, like a "hot time in the old town tonight." We find ourselves thinking of not going to bed yet with this one. We want to respect this person. We want to nurture and bless. Such desires become more than normal courtesy or morality. About this person, we find ourselves fantasizing in noble terms. Some men have treated most dates as objects of sexual desire, and though sexually drawn even more deeply, they find unaccustomed checks rising. Passion is being corralled by something new. We no longer want only to get; we want to give.

Something in us wants to be in a position to give to this woman continually. We want to protect her from then on.

We may discover our spouse by a holy kind of jealousy. Not all jealousy is bad. Solomon saw it as a sign of deep commitment: "Place me like a seal over your heart, like a seal on your arm; for love is as strong as death, its *jealousy* unyielding as the grave" (Song of Sol. 8:6, NIV, emphasis added). Our God is a jealous God (Deut. 5:9). His jealousy is love for us that no other so-called god should have His place. We may discover hurt or jealousy if some other person bids to be the spouse of the one we are considering. By that hurt, not the kind born of our own wounded pride or ego but stemming from concern for the other's welfare, we may recognize love in us for our prospective partner.

It is good for couples to step back and cool off awhile. If it is indeed marital love that God intends, the old saw is quite true that "absence makes the heart grow fonder." We ache when absent from that one. Emotions cool down. Thoughts settle out, but true inner "gnawing" doesn't fade. It grows. We are restless. We feel incomplete and hollow. Finally, we know we can't get along anymore without that one by our side. We may have felt free and "complete" before, but now we sense that since we have found that person, we will never again be full and complete outside of an abiding relationship.

If after the wedding we fail to move into the fullness of marital life, these same feelings of completeness and inner fulfillment may attempt to be expressed in a relationship outside of the marriage. However, what we don't realize is that these feelings really are those that we actually have for our own husband or wife. They are sometimes blocked in our marriage relationship and then transferred where they do not belong. In such a case, the feelings are not wrong, but where we have located their fulfillment is delusory and a trap. They are still the longings of our spirit for fulfillment with our own lifetime spouse.

People often tell me, whether or not another prospective partner has yet appeared, that they are sure they married the wrong one. Perhaps this is so, though I greatly doubt it. After more than fifty years of prayer ministry, I (John) believe I could count on my hands the number of times my discernment has shown that a person truly did marry a wrong choice. The miracle of God's providence continually astonishes me. In the most vehemently quarrelling couples, I still can often feel and see that "rightness."

Whether or not the choice was the best, I know God can make it the most, the highest, and the richest marriage. And that is where our faith should be, that by whatever helter-skelter, fearful-of-failure process He connects us to our spouse, right or wrong, God intends that right there in that union He should prove again that Romans 8:28 is true for every situation in every time in our lives (that all things do work together for good). So our most important counsel is not upon the effort to find just the right one, but that whatever one we do choose, we should set our sails to let God make our marriage the best.

In that way the question is settled. So many get into marriage and then look back, thinking, "I must have made a mistake." Let us settle it beforehand that whatever questions may plague the mind, the heart will be set in God to pay the price to make the most of it. Even should the mind be convinced of error, as my mother said so wisely, "Son, whoever you choose to be your wife, understand that though I love you and will always be your mother, there's no coming home."

For those not yet married, my mother's words should be a warning to walk circumspectly. Scripture says we should not be yoked with unbelievers (2 Cor. 6:14), but that doesn't mean any believer would make a good choice. Remember that a part of our thesis in this book is that it is not necessarily those who believe in mind, or public declaration, who are believers, but those who truly believe in the heart. There may be many who have gone through the ritual of accepting Jesus as Savior who are not yet very much believers in the heart at all.

On the other hand, there are those who, though not professing Christianity, are much more Christian than most Christians! They have all the fruit of the Spirit listed in Galatians 5:22–23. "Surely he will convert eventually," a girl might think to herself. "I just know he's the right one." He may very well be the right one. Don't give up on him automatically just because he hasn't yet converted. He may yet convert. But, as Paul said, "How do you know, O wife, whether you will save your husband? Or how do you know, O husband, whether you will save your wife?" (1 Cor. 7:16). Many men and women live out their whole lives displaying Christian virtues yet never receive Christ. If he is the right one, do not marry unless he converts. "But what if he doesn't?" you might ask. "I might miss the right one." No, you won't. If he does convert, find out whether he is converting to please God or to please you. Don't marry until his motive is right. For if it is not, his newfound "faith" will fade away as quickly as the sound of the wedding bells. Rely on others' discernment about this. When you're in love, your own judgment will be at its weakest.

It is a most tricky business to still the soul (Ps. 131) and wait for the still, small voice of God or to be sure we are not rushing ahead hoping God will bless. Time gives opportunity for the Spirit to still our selfish desires and to make God's will known. Unrest is a most sure sign (not the unrest born of inner gnawing spoken of earlier, but that born of anxiety and tension).

Peace is an indicator. When our intended comes, our heart and mind may flip every which way, while underneath is a peace totally unfamiliar to us. Outside we may be turned every which way but to peace, while inside there is no storm at all. Something has settled. When we are trying to discover, especially concerning one who doesn't yet know the Lord, our logical mind may do convolutions about itself. We may run in endless circles, opposing every thought with its opposite, getting nowhere in a hurry. And yet at the same time there may be a gentle inner knowing. Again, time is the friend of God and man; haste is the enemy. Such inner knowing and resultant calm will stand the test of time; passion and lust will not.

Sometimes lasting friendship is difficult to divide from spouse love, especially since love sometimes enters first by the door of friendship. We often confuse burden-bearing love with romance, or transference with love. All too often prayer ministers think they have "fallen in love" with a person to whom they are ministering. Such relationships might, but seldom do, develop into marital love. Relationships based on need are always unstable and can seldom stand transition into two free equals freely choosing each other. Possessiveness frequently masks itself as love. All the above confusions are best sifted by time. The Holy Spirit is the giver of discernment, but as in healing of the inner man, ripeness is the key to capacity to hear Him. We must be careful not to pluck fruit before it ripens. Perhaps this is another meaning of the warning "I adjure you... that you will not arouse or awaken my love, until she pleases" (Song of Sol. 2:7; 3:5; 8:4—three times the Word uses very similar words!).

It is important to get wise counsel, not only to prevent harm in selecting a husband or wife but also to know what to forgive or confirm in what was the actual process of discovery you went through to find the one you are with. If the ship of your marriage is already on the rocks, your mind may frequently fish for reasons to conclude that the mistake was not in present failures. You want to say, "I must have gotten the wrong one." But by carefully reviewing the process of your heart when you made your choice and spending quiet moments in prayer, the Holy Spirit can assure you and say, "You have the right one; now let's settle down to find out what went wrong." It may be appropriate, depending on the circumstances, to seek out a Christian counselor or a prayer minister who can help you walk through the healing process. They can help you comprehend the art of "finding," for legalities will seldom convince. A prayer minister or Christian counselor who understands the pathways of romantic hearts will have abilities to persuade willful hearts to cease fruitless questions, to let go of alibis and cop-outs, and to settle down to the task of making a go of what is.

LEAVING

Once the prospective partner has been found, a process long underway enters a new phase. From the moment of birth, we enter a pilgrimage from dependence to independence. In the womb every organic, emotional, and spiritual system is totally encased and dependent upon our mothers and fathers. At birth we become our own organic entity. If our own organs do not begin to function without the mother's, death is the result. Independence or leaving is the first and continuing price of ongoing life. As babies, we remain organically dependent—for food, warmth, cleansing, and for every life-sustaining function. We can't do anything for ourselves, except to eat, breathe, sleep, and eliminate, and we are dependent on others for all those things as well. Each lesson we learn is a step toward independence—cessation of breast feeding, toilet training, walking, talking, dressing, accomplishing courtesy, manners, customs, morals, and so on.

As teenagers, we cut some invisible umbilical cords through the individuation and internalization processes, but not all. Some unseen loyalties and belongings that grip our hearts and tie our behavioral responses to parental cues cannot fully be tested and cut until new, more primal loyalties call, and then not merely by presence but by many thousands of incidents and decisions. Each common daily occurrence in marital life calls for further leaving of parents and cleaving to one another.

The greatest and most common difficulty we encounter in ministering to married couples is this matter of leaving and cleaving. Marriage is a three-stage process: "For this cause a man shall *leave* his father and his mother, and shall *cleave* to his wife; and they ["the two," Eph. 5:31] *shall become one flesh*" (Gen. 2:24, emphasis added). If a man or a woman fails to leave father or mother, the second stage cannot happen; they cannot cleave to one another. If leaving and cleaving fail to happen, the third stage cannot even be entered, much less accomplished. They cannot become one flesh.

Leaving is only initially geographical. It is one thing to take the boy off the farm, another to take the farm out of the boy. All the ways a mother does things have set up wishes and demands—a mold in the mind of a man. His wife must become or not be what the mother was—in countless details. More importantly, loyalties, words, ways of command and control, signals and reactions, belongings and self-identifications have been built in relation to the mother that will all need to die if the new relationship is to survive.

Mama calls for assistance in a project, but this evening's plans were already laid with the wife and children. Which is the first priority? Mama of the new bride demands or scolds and advises, but the bride's husband had determined something else. Which ought she follow? Papa insists on correcting his son in front of the son's wife and children. How much loyalty does the son owe? When ought a daughter-in-law speak out? Papa demands that his daughter-in-law or the whole family spend so much time a week at their house. What is true responsibility to honor, and what is too much? Holidays and vacations demand visits home, and battles ensue over which parents are being neglected more often. Papa and Mama keep butting in, saying they have a right, that this is their son or daughter. When does a son or daughter have a right to say, "Bug off; this is my life"? Papa and Mama want to give so many things—money, cars, appliances, and the like. When ought a couple say enough is enough?

When a husband or a wife keeps moving home to Mama, how should a wise parent put a stop to that? Every day daughter calls home and spends hours (seemingly) talking to Mama (or Papa). When is too much too much, and when and how ought a wise parent limit or cut that off? The children keep coming back, asking for financial help. When does wisdom say, "No more," and when and how does compassion bend such rules and help anyway? How much does a secure base aid a marriage—or undermine it?

Each instance must be examined on its own merits, but some guidelines can be firmly set. The first is that each new couple must become their own entity, apart from the parents. They must find life for themselves. They must stand on their own as though colonists on a far planet. New couples and parents must all acknowledge and grant that fact. Once that fact is granted and accomplished both ways, children can come home to visit, and parents can offer help that does not entrap or hinder.

The second guideline involves realization that the job of training the child is done. Parents, you must relinquish the task of shaping, counseling, disciplining, and advising. You no longer have a right to the shaping of decisions. Married couples, you no longer owe parents that kind of obedience! No parent has any position whatsoever to command a married son or daughter! It does not honor to obey your parents rather than your spouse. As an adult, you may decide, in love, to do what your parents ask, but purely by free choice, not by legal, emotional, or any other compulsions. The biblical command to honor one's father and mother no longer involves obedience when married. For the married couple, honoring your parents refers to attitudes and services given in proper priority after duties rendered to spouse and children—not before.

Paula and I would never give a command to any of our six children, all of whom are married and have left the home. That relationship ended upon their arrival at legal age. Unfortunately, many parents think they still have the same position they held when their children were only ten. A drill sergeant may shout at and belittle any recruit in his charge, but the same behavior addressed to his captain may cost him his stripes! Parents must learn that when their children become adults, they are no longer recruits. They have been transferred out of their company and must now be addressed with deference and respect.

The third guideline refers to loyalties and attachments. Husband and wife should say to each other the same words Ruth said to Naomi: "Where you go, I will go, and where you lodge, I will lodge.

Your people shall be my people, and your God, my God" (Ruth 1:16). Attempts by a wife to coerce her husband emotionally to make their residence in her town to be near Papa and Mama are out of place. She must be emotionally free to go wherever he wants her to go, not using her willingness as an emotional clout over his head or as a self-martyring stance. Nor should a husband be drawn by his parents or attempt to coerce his wife to live near his parents.

Parents, your love for your children must always be freely given, and never should it become chains of debt to bind your children to you. If your married children freely choose to be near or to bring the grandchildren often to visit, that is as it should be—a blessing to all. However, you must not trade on past services for present favors, nor should married children allow you to. That day is done. Debts are canceled, as though the day of the wedding is also the day of jubilee.

Jesus gave His all upon the cross. That gift did not bind anyone to Him. He freely gave. Though His was the highest and best gift ever given, it would be an insult to our Lord to think that we therefore owe Him and are controlled by His gifts! His gift did not entrap us. It set us free. Just so, parental love, in everything parents do from conception to maturity, must be seen as freely given, not an entrapment of children from then on.

Couples may want to do things for their parents, especially in their old age, and should feel responsibility to do so from gratitude and a biblical sense of calling. It is God—not parents or laws—who calls couples to care for their parents. It was a delight to give my (John's) father a home in his old age and to have my mother living close to us for a while. But parents ought never to use the past for the present. Having perceived inability in either a couple or their parents to let go and cut umbilical ties, we have some-times advised couples that a distance of five hundred miles may be too close to home and a distance of one thousand miles is better. Whereas couples and parents who have achieved freedom can live next door to each other.

The fourth guideline refers to security—both emotional and financial. Parents need to give a two-edged word: "You can't run home to Papa and Mama," and the opposite, "We'll always be here. You can always come to us." The first means, "You've got to give it your all. You cannot use us to undermine your marriage. Make it out there. And you can't come here unless you've tried it there to your utmost." The second means, "Security is here if everything else fails." Gifts and helps can only be offered to the degree that they do not weaken or undermine, especially the position and confidence of the breadwinner. Most especially, gifts and helps must not be used to entrap the children and make them dependent.

The fifth word concerns preaching and prayers. Perhaps the worst and most destructive continuing pattern between parents and married couples is preaching. Parents must learn not to preach at couples. Couples must learn when and how to say, "Papa (or Mama), this is my life." Couples must learn not to knuckle under to their parents' preachings. Parents no longer have that forum. Wise is a young person who will listen to the counsel of the aged, but there must be freedom and space between them, not control and manipulation. "Old country" parents are often the worst. Descendants of strong cultures have far more difficulty staying clear of untoward parental interference. Some cultures consider it a virtue and traditional parental privilege to harangue and control adult children by the tongue.

Even prayers, soulishly given, can be used to try to control married children. Such prayers as, "Lord, make Sonny be good to his wife," are out of place. We would manage God to manage our children, in ways God wouldn't answer anyway. But the energy of our prayers bothers our children. To pray for them is fine. That is our one continuing duty as parents. Our blessing through prayers is the greatest, most powerful gift we have yet to bestow. But all such come under the guidelines of respect and noninterference. We can only pray successfully in ways that do not interfere, and we can only pray for what does not interfere.

When children are young, they step on our toes. When they are older, they step on our hearts! When they are young, we control. When married, they control their own lives. When older, their hearts and actions sometimes bruise our hearts, but we must have no false shields, no controlling them so we won't hurt so much for them. We must not try to protect our hearts from hurting for them by controlling them to keep them out of trouble. We must not use anything to coercively influence their lives. We stand by, willing and ready to help, but always with reticence, lest that help, even in prayer, would clip their wings.

Finally, concerning grandchildren, all the same guidelines apply. We can give them our love, but the parents must do the shaping and discipline. In our home, grandchildren can come somewhat under our discipline, as we would ask any neighbor's child to abide by our rules when on our property. But in their home, it's hands off. That position belongs only to their parents. If any position is consciously delegated to us by the couple, we must take it with careful deference to their authority. If a couple hosts an overbearing, still-disciplining grandparent, that calls for firmness (respectfully communicated, of course) that if not heeded must terminate the visit. Parents must not allow grandparents to usurp parental position or authority.

All too often, a father visits who has in years past molested his own children. Now the young mother worries, lest he find opportunity to molest his grandchildren. Loyalty to parents and over-compassion for past sins have no priority of any kind over the safety of children! Those children have the fullness of life before them. They are not to be risked for the later years of erstwhile, wayward parents. Under no circumstances should earlier-known molesters be allowed opportunity to be alone with grandchildren! If that cannot easily be safely guaranteed, then visits must be very brief and always with the mother present. We owe no parental debt to risk our children.

It must be assumed, as with alcoholics (that once a person becomes an alcoholic there is always a chance of relapse), that once a molester, always that weakness can overcome again. Our friend Rachel Johnson, at that time the most recognized authority on child abuse in eastern Washington, adamantly stated that apart from Christ, child molesters will do it again. Even if much healing has happened, it is not wise to risk a child alone with such a grand-parent. It is also our experience that men who molest will continue to do so, short of major miracles, and even then they must not be put in places of temptation. If this seems harsh, it is one of the prices for sin that a molesting father must be expected to pay and continue to pay throughout his life as a grandfather. He deserved nothing else than to be cut off (Lev. 18:10, 29)! There is nothing so sacred as the trust God gives a father to protect the sexuality of his daughter, stepdaughter, or granddaughter. One who has violated that trust must serve the consequences without complaint. Mercy and forgiveness must not be allowed to weaken vigilance.

My motive in saying this is not punitive. It is restorative. When a molesting father submits to strict guidelines, it is not punishment. It is restitution, which helps heal the heart of the one he wounded. If I seem repetitious, rigid, or harsh, it is because countless times I have ministered to brokenhearted mothers who were sure their fathers had learned their lesson, only to sob out the story of their discovery of what such men had done to their daughters. Take NO chances. You owe nothing!

Mothers normally have more trouble letting go and not interfering with maturing offspring than do fathers. In old-country homes, sometimes the reverse is true. But in most American homes, the mother finds it more difficult to let alone and keep still. Again, let us say, couples, you need to learn how to be gently and firmly incisive with such mothers. It is kindness to say firmly and compassionately, "Mom, you have nothing more to say in this matter. I am a grown person. Your job ended the day I married. You are interfering. Please stop." If a word to the wise is sufficient, well and good. It is still kindness to say to the persisting, "Mom, we must respectfully ask you to leave." It is not kindness to a mother to let her become a disturbance in your family. False guilt says, "After all the trouble you gave her, can't you put up with a little from her?" Perhaps you alone could and should, but you are not alone, and your wife (or husband) and children are your first priority. They gave her no trouble in your childhood and should not now be required to pay whatever penalty you think you still owe! If they can put up with her, it will be good for them to make that sacrifice, but if she is too great a disturbance, the present family is first priority, and she must go.

As a prayer minister, I repeat this matter also so firmly because I would have no hesitancy to say that a great proportion of marriages that fail do so because one or both partners refused to or could not leave home! Leaving is an absolute prerequisite to cleaving. There can be no cleaving to the marital partner whatsoever so long as one or both parents occupy the place of the spouse in the heart. It takes years in the best of circumstances for hearts to transfer willingly from parents to spouse. I still automatically wrote my parents' address as my home address on job applications several years after Paula and I were married!

Cleaving

Cleaving is a matter of decision, not once but again and again, to commit our lives to our spouses—"I am not single; I am corporate." Marital love is not romantic feelings but commitment in daily responsible acts. Cleaving is a matter of choice, in little daily incidents requiring sacrifice, again and again, year in and year out.

Whereas leaving was a matter of closing (closing the heart and mind to continuing inappropriate parental influence), cleaving is a matter first of opening to one's spouse, then closing to all others. It is by God's wisdom that most marriage ceremonies include: "And keep thee only unto him (or her)." To keep our hearts open to our husband or wife and closed to all others is the great art of marriage, not only sexually but also in countless areas of sharing. Cleaving is the primary calling and task of honorable marriage. Only Paula has the full right of unquestioned access to my holy of holies. Only Paula has the right to a full, no-secret relationship. She alone has full security clearance. Cleaving is a matter of holding open to her no matter what the pain and holding shut to all others in all areas of sharing that belong only to her, no matter what seeming blessedness allures me to give to another what belongs only to Paula.

Marriage is an ongoing process to a fullness of blessedness. All couples stop off now and then to rest on this or that plateau. All too few keep going on to fullness of blessedness.

Fullness is a union of mind and heart in which neither has been obliterated or stunted and both have become all that each can become, enhanced and fulfilled by the other. Neither could have come to fullness apart from the other, but neither was kept from it by the other. Fullness is a rhythm, a dance, a musical duet, spontaneous and free, yet ordered and regular. Each could stand alone but chooses not to, and in the choosing, something greater than addition of one plus one has happened.

Forgiveness and the cross are central to two becoming one, because no one can stand the fires of conflict in union without grace. Hurt engenders hurt, and response demands response, both by psychology and the law of sowing and reaping. On the cross Jesus reaps what our evil sowings demand and sets us free to reap the fullness of blessings. We cannot be truly subject to one another unless we are first subject to Him (Eph. 5:21).

In the Garden of Eden God created man and woman for one another. The marriage state was the state of creation! Adam and Eve knew no childhood apart from one another! Eve knew no life at all apart from Adam! We are only told of creation and then union.

Together they had work to do. Labor to dress the garden and to keep it was not an added condition, or a fallen one, but the blessed condition of creation. (See Genesis 2:15.) The Fall did not create labor; it only gave it tension and sweat. So the fullness of re-creation in Jesus is not idleness but harness together in labor, without tension and sweat. (See Genesis 3:17–19.) It is our contention that no couple comes to fullness of union apart from labor. "For we are His workmanship, created in Christ Jesus for good works, which God prepared beforehand, that we should walk in them" (Eph. 2:10). Our vocation is *our* vocation, not something one or both happened to find to do, but something planned by God as ours from the ground plan of our creation for one another.

A job is not a vocation. A vocation is a calling, from the Latin *vocare*, which means "to call." Tent making was a job that allowed St. Paul to respond to his calling as an apostle. A vocation may also be a person's job, in which case the couple is doubly blessed. But a married person's vocation is by definition not singular. Though they may be performing separate physical tasks, the attitude of heart is not to be singular. Each separate task is to contribute to unity and harmony in a corporate goal larger than any job. It was in the context of Adam's vocation that God saw that it was not good for man to be alone, and so He said, "I will make an help meet for him" (Gen. 2:18, KJV). A vocation is a calling from God, for which that man was created—and his wife with him! A married man who tries to do his task alone is in jeopardy. Such loneliness culminates, so, as we have seen, hundreds of men have fallen into adultery because some woman (secretary, working mate) seemed to fulfill that part of him that needed his vocational helpmeet.

Both may not recognize the calling to vocation at once, or even for many years. They are blessed if they do, but perseverance and circumspect walking must pertain until both do. It is in the context of vocation that a couple shall come to fullness of oneness, and not apart from it, for that is their purpose and destiny in creation.

Every couple has a vocation whether they realize it or not. Many may be doing it and never have given it the name. It need not ring with recognized holiness. What seemed spiritual or holy about tilling a garden? God calls men and women to be farmers, educators, homemakers, publishers, merchants, and so on. For some, garbage collecting is a job; for some the same is also their vocation. Anything can be done with the backing and artistry of heaven. For some, even to be a governor of a state may be only a job, while fulfillment of vocation is in their children or in tending their bed of roses in the garden. Who knows what any other man's vocation is? It is best if a man and wife know it consciously and respond so together, but blessedness and fullness of union arrive anyway if they simply get in harness together.

The reward of heaven is never said to be clouds of fleece, suggesting laziness and rest, but greater labors:

> And the one who had received the five talents came up and brought five more talents, saying, "Master, you entrusted five talents to me; see, I have gained five more talents." His master said to him, "Well done, good and faithful slave; you were faithful with a few things, I will put you in charge of many things, enter into the joy of your master." The one also who had received the two talents came up and said, "Master, you entrusted to me two talents; see, I have gained two more talents." His master said to him, "Well done, good and faithful slave; you were faithful with a few things, I will put you in charge of many things; enter into the joy of your master."
>
> —MATTHEW 25:20–23

Not only is it that a man and woman come into fullness of life by joining hands in this life in vocation, but it is also by that vocation that God has designed to prepare them for service in the next life in heaven. The plan of marriage is to make a deposit in the soul beyond the portals of death. Marriage itself ends at death. But we do "take it with us." That which we take is what we have become—intellectually, emotionally, and spiritually. Whatever we have become has happened in relationship to our spouse in our service to God and man. That shape of character, that mind of memories we are, goes with us to our next labors in heaven. That is the end of marriage and the fullness of becoming one, to become that peculiar, distinct kind of flower God has planned to pluck for whatever bouquets He forms in heaven.

CHAPTER 5

STRENGTH IN ONENESS

Be subject to one another in the fear of Christ. Wives, be subject to your own husbands, as to the Lord. For the husband is the head of the wife, as Christ also is the head of the church, He Himself being the Savior of the body. But as the church is subject to Christ, so also the wives ought to be to their husbands in everything. Husbands, love your wives, just as Christ also loved the church and gave Himself up for her; that He might sanctify her, having cleansed her by the washing of water with the word, that He might present to Himself the church in all her glory, having no spot or wrinkle or any such thing; but that she should be holy and blameless. So husbands ought also to love their own wives as their own bodies. He who loves his own wife loves himself; for no one ever hated his own flesh, but nourishes and cherishes it, just as Christ also does the church, because we are members of His body. For this cause a man shall leave his father and mother, and shall cleave to his wife; and the two shall become one flesh.

—EPHESIANS 5:21–31

Then Jesus said to His disciples, "If anyone wishes to come after Me, let him deny himself, and take up his cross, and follow Me. For whoever wishes to save his life shall lose it; but whoever loses his life for My sake shall find it."

—MATTHEW 16:24–25

The problem of becoming one is self-centered selfishness. Behind all the troubles ever spoken and written about is one malady common to all mankind—simple, self-centered selfishness. The common sin of all mankind is to look out continually for number one! Its opposite is not a self-sacrificing, kind, and giving person. Generous, kind, and compassionate people may still be motivated by self. We do not overcome self simply by developing a practiced lifestyle of generosity—though that would help. Selfishness is not coterminous with stinginess. It does not mean merely someone who will not give of himself, share what he has, or do for others. It means one who is "self-ish," who lives in and for his own self-definition, whether doing good for others or being what we usually recognize as selfish.

Generous people are usually well liked in society. Everyone naturally expects them to do well in marriage. Sometimes that is so, but not always, because it is precisely in married life that selfish self-centeredness is most impossible to continue to mask. Our spouse lives as no one else behind the front society sees and encounters as no other the raw core of our flesh.

Self-centered selfishness is the final taproot of disease crucially destructive to the full flowering of oneness. We cannot become fully corporate so long as self still governs.

The problem of becoming one is fear—fear to die: "...who through fear of death were all their lifetime subject to bondage" (Heb. 2:15, KJV). The death we fear is death to fleshly self-control. We are afraid to let go of those structures of self, those practices of character and personality, by which we think we have met and controlled our life and situations and people around us.

"Truly, truly, I say to you, unless a grain of wheat falls into the earth and dies, it remains by itself alone; but if it dies, it bears much fruit" (John 12:24). Until we die to that self by which we have attempted to control life, all primary people around us are subconsciously viewed as satellites in our orbit. So long as others around us remain in place, fulfilling our picture of the way life should go, we can be at rest and let them be at peace. But when they threaten our practiced way of life, life becomes uncomfortable and we do whatever we think we must in order to move them back into orbit—command, wheedle, threaten, scold, manipulate, comfort, hit, "love up on," give the silent treatment, harangue, and so on. We do anything that hopefully will return loved ones to the status quo, in a continuum from "soft and gentle ways" to raging tantrums, most often unaware that what compels us is not the loving concern for others we think it is (which we often trumpet loudly) but is actually the kingdom of self. We remain alone even if surrounded by people because no one wants to be controlled. No one is willing to become a mere satellite in our orbit. We have to die to self to become safe to be corporate.

CONTROLLED BY SUBMISSION

Some husbands or wives surrender themselves to the other's picture of life. A wife may submissively act out her husband's every wish. She may think that is what Ephesians 5:22 commands her to do. Many off-balance teachings about submission may buttress that stance. It seems, then, that she is the one who has totally denied herself and given herself in true, self-sacrificial love to her husband. Not necessarily so, however. In fact, it may be that she has first found a way of copping out from becoming herself and, second, only a more subtle way of controlling.

Her submissive role may actually be a way of controlling her environment. It makes for peace (the lifeless peace and quiet of a rock) while preventing her from presenting to her husband the more risky enterprise of a lively and vivacious helpmeet who could fulfill him. She becomes an extension of him rather than an adequate counterpart. By learning what pleases him and by always doing it, she controls him. Outwardly he may be pleased, while inwardly he is dying.

A husband may serve his wife faithfully, but that is just it, he may be serving rather than meeting her as a person. As a boy he may have learned to quiet his mother by compliance; consequently he placates and controls by performing whatever will keep the peace. Such a man may have unconsciously learned to pander to whichever emotion causes a wife to curl up and purr. Such men may seem to be ideal husbands. It may be difficult for a wife of such an "ideal" husband to identify the problem; she just knows she is unhappy. Something isn't fulfilled. Wives of milquetoast husbands usually become angrier and more demanding the more slavishly their husbands perform. Unconsciously, they are trying to provoke their husbands to angrily break out of the mold, to make them take charge of life and be the head of their house.

Sometimes control is established not by subtle ways of kindness but by force, angriness, or loudness. That type of control is easily recognized for what it is. But it is not that much more easily broken. We tend to think of such people as strong personalities: "I'm afraid to buck him; he's so strong." In reality, behind the mad bluff is a fearful little child who has learned to control his world by making others jump.

Whatever the method of control, the cause is the same—self. The result is the same—failure of full corporate life and wholeness.

TRUE SUBMISSION THROUGH ONENESS

St. Paul gave us the one successful route to married life: "Be subject to one another in the fear of Christ" (Eph. 5:21). That is a simple maxim, an absolute law of marital relationship, which could be stated, "Unless you are subject to Jesus Christ, you cannot be subject to one another." Or, "If you are not dead to self in Christ, you cannot die to self in relation to others," or its opposite, "Only if you are alive in the Holy Spirit, to give life to others as Jesus gives, can you give life to one another." The opposite is also a law of human behavior. Whoever is not subject to the Lord Jesus Christ (close enough to change his character) *will* be subject to the flesh of others rather than to blessedness. Only as our Lord's identification with us brings our world of self to death on the cross, only as His Holy Spirit empowers us to live outside of and beyond the walls of self in and for Him, does true life emerge in any capacity— and most especially in marriage.

True oneness happens not by obliteration of one for the other nor by expansion of one's self over the other, but it happens by death to self in Christ until motives and urges arise out of His nature in us. "He must increase, but I must decrease" (John 3:30). It is not, as many have often mistakenly quoted, "I must decrease, but He must increase." That inverts God-given order for death and rebirth. If I attempt to decrease, that remains only another ploy of self. Only as He increases, by His choice, by His initiative upon me, does that successfully call my self to death. Only as His life arises within me does something else and more than self become the motivating force that enables. Nor is it that His life obliterates me. His self-death is so complete that the more I die to me and rise in Him, the more I become the fullness of me. I do not become a cookie-cutter copy of Jesus Christ. I become the fullness God created me to be, only I can take no credit, no pride, no boasting for what I am (1 Cor. 1:31). Nor do I have to defend it, live for it, or keep it going. That's His job. I simply live in Him for Him, and He lives in me for me.

Fullness of death and of new life causes a spouse to sense by the Spirit what the other wants and needs. That sensing does not pander to the flesh; it does not satisfy lusts or baser motives. We learn to read by the Spirit what in wisdom is good for our spouse and to act accordingly. Oneness, then, is not obliteration or control of each other but the freshness of two children of God delighting in a world of discovery and adventure in blessing as we seek to bless and fulfill one another and all others. Our hearts sing together. Our minds are in tune so that tiniest clues catch to a symphony of thought and concerted action. One aim, one purpose, to live to bless others, ties all things in a concert of unity. Spirits so embrace and interflow that physical coordination enhances and ease of rhythm and action refreshes rather than tires, whatever the work-load in harness together. Oneness becomes a symphonic harmony of two individuals freely being themselves, spontaneous and open, yet interwoven as one melody of service and worship. Oneness is not a loss of individualism, as though the corporate mass had swallowed up and ingested each one. It is more like two glowing embers in one common fire or a tenor and an alto singing to individual fullness in a choir.

FLESHLY UNITY

The problem of oneness frequently involves fleshly striving to create it. Oneness is not something we should directly strive for, watch over, and measure, and thereby become tense about. It is a result, a by-product of life in Christ. The antidote to fractures is therefore not to strive to return to oneness—which would result mainly in judging and measuring and so falling further apart—but turning back to worship, to serve the Lord, unmindful of self. Oneness returns as He returns.

A group of us formed a cell group. We wanted to enter into oneness, sharing problems and joys, praying for one another daily. We entered into covenants, only to be filled, like any couple after the honeymoon, with dissensions and battles. Then the Lord revealed that our lack of oneness was due to fleshly striving. Along the way, He pointed out that every attempt of men to get together He Himself has frustrated. He reminded us that the Tower of Babel was an attempt in unity that He Himself prevented, after which He confused the tongues of men and scattered them (Gen. 11:1–9). He revealed to us that it was He Himself, not satanic power, who had so moved men as to cripple the League of Nations, the United Nations, and so on. Whenever in history men have attempted unity by the flesh, He Himself has broken them apart and scattered them.

We cried out, "How then are we to become a corporate body?"—having become so acutely aware by then of our divisive flesh. He answered by a vision given to one member of our prayer group during prayer. This person saw a green pasture in which all the sheep were crowding to be near the shepherd. The Lord then said, "As you seek Me first, as each one strives to be near Me, you are naturally drawn closer to one another. Anything else perverts the God-given order and results in division."

Corporateness in marriage (in church or anywhere else) comes by seeking Him first. Where He is not the head, selfishness resurrects (if it ever died), and division soon follows.

> For where jealousy and selfish ambition exist, there is disorder and every evil thing. But the wisdom from above is first pure, then peaceable, gentle, reasonable, full of mercy and good fruits, unwavering, without hypocrisy. And the seed whose fruit is righteousness is sown in peace by those who make peace.
>
> —JAMES 3:16–18

One partner may not actively be seeking Him. But the unbelieving partner is consecrated through the believing partner (1 Cor. 7:14), so a lack in one partner need not prevent unity and oneness in heart.

The problem of becoming one is the constant difficulty of forgiveness. Someone has said that marriage is a twenty-four-hour-a-day practice in the art of forgiveness. Unintended sleights happen as frequently as flies gather to crumbs, to say nothing of intended hurts. But so often we are not enough aware that we are being hurt so as to do something about it, until our head of steam erupts somewhere. Or knowing, we can't quite catch hold of the frazzled ends of emotions and events to tie them successfully to the cross and so get it all done with. Eruption of fights is commonly a barometer of our distance from Jesus, for had we walked closely enough, then 1 John 1:7 would have been fulfilled in us: "But if we walk in the light as He Himself is in the light, we have fellowship with one another, and the blood of Jesus His Son cleanses us from all sin." We are then relegated to 1 John 1:9. We need to confess our sins, because only outward confession aloud to one another can restore unity. The prevention of hassles is devotion, but the only antidote is confession and forgiveness.

The problem of oneness is a loss of vision and purpose. When goals no longer call us beyond self, our primal, fleshly purpose (to get rather than to give) is resurrected, and we reecho the common song of demand and refusal. Purpose is restored only as we return to harness. Thinking and talking about it leads only to affixing blame and erecting defenses. Serving Jesus, without a word (1 Pet. 3:1–2), is the simple sole answer.

THE TRUTH ABOUT ONENESS THROUGH CHRIST

Oneness is not the end. It is the condition by which we get there. The cause is Jesus. The end is fulfillment of life, purpose, and destiny. Oneness is walking hand in hand; destiny is where we are going.

Oneness is marked by laughter and ease of heart. Trust flourishes within it. Trust is not that the other will not fail. Trust is that God will bring good and that all participants will recover from whatever error(s) may threaten. Trust is patience, that I am not called quickly to straighten out the other or myself lest all be lost. Trust is forbearance, that the other's or my own fumbles or purposeful sins are but momentary and require only my love, compassion, and forgiveness.

Only in oneness are we truly capable of rejoicing in the other's accomplishments. Prior to fullness of death of self, we only think we rejoice, while inwardly we grind our teeth in jealousy and feelings of inferiority. The arrival of oneness is the purchase of highest fulfillment for us when the other does better than we, for on the one hand we know we are part of the support system that enables, and on the other his success has become ours because we are one. "The works that I do shall he do also; and greater works than these shall he do" (John 14:12). This becomes our aim and our joy rather than our dread of replacement. Then it is joy in the happiness of others that arises from innermost wells; it does not have to be trumped up, and its end is not a sour taste in the mouth and despondency but contentment and a sense of well-being.

Oneness is also marked by grief. More than our emotions grieve when someone who is one with us is hurt. Sorrow weeps deep within our spirit and breaks to the surface. Hurtful as it is, such sorrow has a sweetness about it, having been born of love for the other (Eccles. 7:2–8). Such sorrow sometimes arrives long before conscious knowledge of the event, because in the faculties of our spirits we sense more than our minds know. It becomes relief then to know what it is we have been sorrowing about. Knowledge directs sorrow to effective action, such as prayer or comforting the loved one, but it adds no dread. There is a joy that undergirds godly sorrow for another (Eccles. 7:2–8; 2 Cor. 7:10).

We pop in and out of oneness, like a hat continually blowing off in a high wind. It is the resurgent demands of resurrecting flesh, the strident stentorian calls of self, which are the wind of loss. But it is Jesus who restores us, again and again, always one more time than we have fallen. The problem with becoming one comes when we don't let Him restore us. Pride is thus the essential quality of ineptitude, the obstinate and adamant factor of walls in our flesh. In the end, when everything else is said and done, it is pride that rules the empire of selfish self-centeredness and continually locates its grave to dig up some means to puff it to life again.

"Humble yourselves, therefore, under the mighty hand of God, that He may exalt you at the proper time, casting all your anxiety upon Him, because He cares for you" (1 Pet. 5:6–7). The Greek word for *casting* actually means "to hurl with great force," as when casting a javelin. Oneness is therefore a condition kept by vehemently hurling our fears to God. For it is fear that induces pride. When we feel empty or threatened, insecure or put down, pride is the false comforter who puffs up our deflated balloon. When we are full of His worth as our worth, we have no need to puff up, brag, or defend. Thus we can "be of the same mind toward one another; do not be haughty in mind, but associate with the lowly. Do not be wise in your own estimation" (Rom. 12:16). The antidote for pride is not to try to be humble. That way we only replay the game of self. To humble oneself under the hand of God is to praise Him in the midst of difficulty, to give glory and honor and majesty unto Him. That effectually humbles us. To confess our sin instead of the other's sin, especially when it is the other who has hurt us and who is so obviously wrong, humiliates our pride. To seek out our own root of bitterness deprives pride of its self-justifying stances. In short, humbling the self is best accomplished by seeking death to self on the cross.

Transformation is never complete. We are always much like the man who was given a medal for humility only to have it taken away because he wore it! To consider others as being better than ourselves (Phil. 2:3) is a sign of humility, but we only do that as something other than a game of self when we are truly crushed by the realization of our own sin (Ps. 34:18). Paradoxically, it is primarily when the blessedness of oneness takes place that our spirits gain the strength to try something to break out of successive hidden walls of self. So, strangely, it is oneness that often precedes, one might even say precipitates, rash attempts that lead to failures and fractures. That is one reason why we pop in and out of oneness. Each touch of blessedness gives grace to attempt the next level of maturation, with all its attendant risks, threats, failures, and pride.

Oneness is therefore neither static nor boring. It is a prelude to leaps off cliffs! We cannot usually take leaps of faith without gaining courage to try. Courage comes first by God's grace, but that grace is most commonly mediated to us through human unity.

Oneness is therefore a flickering candlelight in the wind, deceptively strong, for as often as trouble puffs it out, it relights, kindled by the fire of God's love.

Oneness is the ground in which transformation produces maturity, both in marriage and in the body of Christ as a whole.

> And He gave some as apostles, and some as prophets, and some as evangelists, and some as pastors and teachers, for the equipping of the saints for the work of service, to the building up of the body of Christ; until we all attain to the unity of the faith, and of the knowledge of the Son of God, to a mature man, to the measure of the stature which belongs to the fulness of Christ.
>
> —EPHESIANS 4:11–13

CHAPTER 6

TOWARD SEXUAL WHOLENESS: BECOMING CHRISTLIKE IN OUR HUMANNESS

Let your fountain be blessed, and rejoice in the wife of your youth. As a loving hind and a graceful doe, let her breasts satisfy you at all times; be exhilarated always with her love.

—PROVERBS 5:18–19

So husbands ought also to love their own wives as their own bodies. He who loves his own wife loves himself; for no one ever hated his own flesh, but nourishes and cherishes it, just as Christ also does the church.

—EPHESIANS 5:28–29

For this is the will of God, your sanctification; that is, that you abstain from sexual immorality; that each of you know how to possess his own vessel in sanctification and honor, not in lustful passion, like the Gentiles who do not know God; and that no man transgress and defraud his brother in the matter because the Lord is the avenger in all these things, just as we also told you before and solemnly warned you. For God has not called us for the purpose of impurity, but in sanctification.

—1 THESSALONIANS 4:3–7

God designed us to enjoy sex. He united our sensitive spirits to delicately intricate, wondrously strong, feeling bodies to give us great heights of blessing and joy in sexual union. There is nothing we can do with one another through our bodies that is so holy and perfectly fulfilling as marital sexual union. God meant it for refreshment, fulfillment, recreation, realignment, release, sharing, procreation, healing, lessons in loving, practice in sensitivities, development in the art of laying down our lives for another, completion, entrance into the kingdom of being corporate, gratitude, longing, hope, endurance, fun, laughter, mysticism, embrace, and so on through endless catalogs of blessing. It is perhaps God's best physical gift to mankind. Precisely because it possesses so much power to bless, mankind to that degree can warp and twist sex to unleash destructive power.

Sexual blessedness, more than any other form of human encounter, depends upon our being fully human. *A human being is a person who has a loving, awakened, and sensitive personal spirit by which he empathizes with others and cherishes others more than himself.* We do not remain human simply by existing. Our humanness must be nurtured through copious affection in infancy, enabling us to be thus drawn forth to love. A human baby is the only animal in all of creation who will not become his own kind if not raised by his own kind. A dog raised among cats will still behave like a dog. A horse raised among cows will not act like a cow. But a human raised among wolves (as has happened in history) will run on all fours and bay at the moon (if not found and retrained soon enough). We have to be loved to love, talked with to talk, trained to respond socially. We do not learn these things by instinct as animals do. We are necessarily societal, dependent on our parents longer than any other species in all creation. This means that our reactions to our parents and our society form our character generally in our childhood, and specifically in the way we will relate to others sexually in adulthood. Sexual blessedness depends upon the capacity of our spirits to reach through our bodies to nurture, bless, enfold, enrich, and enrapture the heart and spirit of another. That capacity is activated, nurtured, and disciplined by our relation to our fathers and mothers. Before we are six, the ability to later enjoy sex fully has either been enabled or destroyed. Failing to receive from our fathers especially, we cannot enter into the fullness of what ought to be. Aberrational forms subsequently await us like reefs under the shallow waters of our living.

To become human means (at most) to become like Jesus.* Jesus was the one fully human person. We use the word wrongly

---

* We do not speak here of humanism, which is Satan's copy, by which man is prompted to elevate himself and his supposed rights, but of our Lord's work in bringing forth His sons and daughters on Earth.

when we say, "I did that [bad thing] because I am only human."
No, we did that wrong thing purely because we are inhuman. If
we were human we would do as Jesus did! We would be compassionate, warm, open, giving, embracing, and nurturing. Our spirit,
perfectly wedded to our body, would rejoice to embrace another
for His sake rather than ours alone. That life of living to bless others
would be so natural and fulfilling to us that we would be willing,
like Jesus, to suffer loss for the happiness of another. That sacrificial willingness is the quintessence of success in marital sexual
union, for only as both husband and wife are willing to give all
they are through their bodies to fulfill the other can either or both
reach the fullness of blessedness in sex.

To become human means (at least) to become capable of empa-
thizing with another. It means to have a functioning spirit that
through our bodily senses can commiserate or rejoice with another.
It means ability to hurt empathetically for another. Concerning
conscience, it means to hurt in advance for our brother, lest our
brother be hurt by what we have to do. Thus the first indicator
of the ability to be human is to have a working conscience. The
essence of humanity is told by conscience. When we do not have a
functioning spirit filled with love, we cannot care how our brother
feels, nor do we feel bad if we happen to be the one who causes
him harm. To be inhuman is to be dead to concern for the welfare
of our fellow man. Witness the vicious acts of street gangs and the
lack of conscience among increasing numbers of fatherless children today (2 Tim. 3:1–5). We are born possessing a spirit. But
our spirit does not yet know how to love another. That capacity
must be awakened, brought forth, instructed, and disciplined.
The task of nurture and discipline is spoken specifically to fathers,
"Fathers…bring them up in the discipline and instruction of

the Lord" (Eph. 6:4). Mothers give life and nurture. Fathers are primarily responsible to call forth life and shape it.

The capacity to be sexual as an adult is formed in a girl as her spirit learns to nestle safely into the strength of her father's arms. As she romps and plays, rocks with him in his chair on his lap, curls up on his chest, and delights him with her, she learns what it is to bless and be blessed, to trust herself restfully into the hands of a man, to let her spirit flow into another's and back again. She learns how to let her spirit come alive in the embrace of another of the opposite sex. A wife who has never been allowed such life with her father may not be able to reach a climax in sex, because the high moments of climax require letting go control of herself into her husband, and she can't do that. She may enjoy the physical titillations of sexual union, but the glory is far from her because that capacity has never been aroused to function. She may never even know she has missed what God intended. Only one who has tasted mountain air can truly be aware that the muggy heaviness of river bottom atmosphere is not all there is to breathing.

The capacity for a man to be sexual is formed in the same way. Though he may drink proportionately more identification of himself sexually from his mother than a daughter does, the capacity and shape of his spirit to meet and embrace is formed by his life with his father. Hugs, romps, rides on the shoulders, walks in the fields, banter and laughter, mock fights, and games teach his spirit the shape of responses to others. The way his father embraces or keeps distant from his mother soaks into a growing boy as his definition of how to be a man with a woman. The way a father gives sympathy or jumps to false conclusions, the way he empathizes with hurt or shouts obscenities for weakness, the way he touches with gentle hand or slaps with violence—countless such daily experiences write upon a growing boy how his spirit should express itself through his body and character.

God intended for fathers to teach their sons and daughters the blessedness of sex and the warnings we need to keep us away from immorality. Read Proverbs, chapters 1–7, especially Proverbs 5:1–5:

> My son, give attention to my wisdom,
> Incline your ear to my understanding;
> That you may observe discretion,
> And your lips may reserve knowledge,
> For the lips of an adulteress drip honey,
> And smoother than oil is her speech;
> But in the end she is bitter as wormwood,
> Sharp as a two-edged sword.
> Her feet go down to death,
> Her steps lay hold of Sheol.

A tree cannot grow roots into the air and leaves under the ground. We have sense enough to know that God has firmly fixed certain things to develop only in particular times and ways. Nor would we try to run a car on its top and hope the wheels could spin on air fast enough to move us somewhere. We have sense enough to know that even the things man makes must abide by law, or they won't operate. Strangely, however, Bible-believing Christians can get it into their heads that God didn't mean it when He said, "Thou shalt not commit adultery!" Scientifically we know that all machines must be operated in obedience to law, or they plug up or explode. Nutritionally we know that some things are poison to the body, no matter what we may feel or think about them. How then did we become so blind as not to see that all manner of sexual diseases run rampant wherever people practice sex without God-given right and not where husband and wife share sex in the beauty of a God-sanctioned relationship? Ought not that fact alone be enough to convince our foolish minds of the reality of God's laws? "And receiving in their own persons the due penalty of their error" (Rom. 1:27).

Every one of us must know without a shadow of doubt the irrevocable, unbendable absoluteness of God's laws. He meant what He said, exactly as He said it, to ensure for us the blessedness of His gift. It is not that He gave the "thou shalt nots" to keep us from having fun, but that we might truly enjoy the fullness He created us to have.

Sex outside of marriage absolutely can have no blessedness! It is God's Holy Spirit that sings through our spirit the love song of the universe in sex; the Holy Spirit will not flow in forbidden places! Not only is sex outside of marriage, any form of marital sex between any other than husband with wife, sin and loss, but it is also degradation of God's creation, insult to Him, rebellion, and foolishness. Never should we upon hearing confession of sexual sin say, "Oh, that's all right," or "Don't feel so guilty." Nor should we ever counsel another, "Try it. It will help you get over your inhibitions." That is abomination before God. Though God looks on the heart and circumstances with compassion and forgiveness, there are no exceptions whatsoever to the moral laws of God.

Behind many sexual sins or aberrations is some form of ruination or blockage in childhood. We should allow the Holy Spirit to dig for root causes. We may even be led to find a Christian counselor or prayer minister to help us, whose mind is keen-edged with the sword of God's Word.

Said the other way around, perhaps no one would ever fall into an aberration or sexual sin if he were truly human and capable. His spirit's conscience would sing out so loudly and strongly, he would turn in revulsion before committing the act. But we are not that human or capable. Perhaps for compassion's sake we who minister should remember that we are more sinned against than sinning—we being but one and there being many to corrupt us.

In this chapter we want to deal primarily, however, not with the present fact of sexual sin but with incidents and structures formed in early life that create the fertile ground for transgression. By uncovering these structures in our pasts and being healed, we can become fit for the glorious future our Lord has prepared for us.

Behind any sexual aberration or sin is a flawed character. Let us settle it as a rule: no whole person falls into sexual sin (1 John 3:9)! Sexual sin, however enticing to our flesh, is abhorrent to our spirit. We do not naturally gravitate to sexual sin as whole people in Christ, but away from it. If the flow of our desires continually pulls us to sexual sin, that comes from a bad root in us. Good trees do not produce bad fruit; bad ones do (Matt. 7:17).

We posit all this in the beginning to end once and for all the lying notion we, as prayer ministers, have heard so often: "Well, I couldn't help it. I just fell in love." Or, "I guess I love her too much to stay away from her." Or, "If you love someone, why, of course it couldn't be sin, could it?" Nonsense! Rot and deception! Love does no wrong thing! Good trees do not produce bad fruit. Lust, a flawed character, death of conscience apart from Christ, and deception produce sin. Whoever commits fornication or adultery did not fall in love; he fell into hate. If love was the starting point, what followed became use and manipulation. Human love alone would have respected the sanctity of the other. God's love in the couple would have respected God and His laws and the sanctity of the other's soul and body. Whoever commits sexual sin flaunts all that is holy for egocentric, selfish reasons. Let us once and for all strip off the romantic, excusing, glossing-over veneer. Immorality is ugly, not beautiful. Destructive, not freeing. Disgusting, not ennobling. Hateful, not loving. Indescribable loss of the holy that has been given of God privately to only two, not fulfilling.

Pornography and R-rated and X-rated movies do not glorify sex; they denigrate it. Quantity of sexual involvement does not fulfill an individual outside the marriage bed; it empties him and leaves him feeling hollow. No one who has never married has ever had true sex, no matter how many affairs he has had, no matter what reputation he possesses as a "lover." He is not a lover; he is a self-centered little boy playing falsely at being a man.

Legend has it that Don Juan, famous for 1,003 sexual affairs, was offered only a jester's jacket by Satan in hell. "What?" he protested. "I'm no fool. I was a great lover." Satan offered him a bargain. If he could recognize and remember just one of his many "loves," he would not have to assume the fool's cloak. One by one, his romantic partners came before him. He failed to remember even one. At last he had to admit it. He had not been a lover, only a fool. The jacket was appropriately his to wear for all eternity.

No man who is truly a lover ever *uses* another. No man who truly loves embraces the bosom of one who is not his wife (Prov. 5:18–20). No man who truly loves demolishes the glory God designed for blessing for only one other person.

> For this is the will of God, your sanctification; that is, that you abstain from sexual immorality; that each of you know how to possess his own vessel [make love to his own wife] in sanctification and honor, not in lustful passion, like the

> Gentiles who do not know God; and that no man transgress
> and defraud his brother in the matter.
>
> —1 THESSALONIANS 4:3–6

To enter another man's wife is to defraud him of the glory God has given only to him: "An excellent wife is the crown of her husband, but she who shames him is as rottenness in his bones" (Prov. 12:4).

Today's young people are being barraged with a Niagara of lies through countless media—movies, novels, newspapers, magazines, comic strips, periodicals, false counselors and teachers, radio, TV, popular music, gossip columns, and so on, all proclaiming that sex is OK anywhere, anytime. Or worse, perhaps quasi-morally, "It's all right if you're in love." The worst part of the flood is often parental example—separations, subsequent dating, divorces, the infidelities children see or sense, even false sexual partners sometimes brought into the home behind not-too-closed doors. I (John) often think the flood Satan pours out of his mouth (note, from his mouth) after the woman (in Revelation 12:15) may be nothing other than the floods of sexual, immoral, and theological "verbal garbage" men continually spew out, especially in this generation.

FORNICATION

Fornication is sexual intercourse before marriage. The cause is not the above-mentioned flood, which may indeed bid to sweep away an otherwise moral young person. But the primary fact is that if a person is strong and whole in Jesus, he can and will stand. "In a flood of great waters they shall not reach him" (Ps. 32:6). Our purpose here is not to deal with surface pressures but to minister to the root reasons for falling. Piaget, a French sociologist, states the root reason: If a person keeps himself virginal sexually, he (or she) loves and respects his (or her) father and mother. If a person commits fornication, he (or she) hates and/or disrespects father and/or mother.

Many times people have come to us who have committed fornication a number of years earlier. They have confessed privately and to others and have heard the words of forgiveness, but they still feel guilty and unclean. The questions we ask them soon uncover the fact that their sexual sin was not isolated but was connected to other things. There may have been anger and rebellion toward parents or a need to throw oneself away to prevent one's parents from rejoicing in their child's glory. Or a hunger for a father's love, so that the touch of a man became so tonic that a "no" could not be spoken. Or a need to punish the parents. Or simply the lack of a functioning conscience because the father had never been there. Or a need to prove again and again that men, or women, are "like that" (like their judgment against one or both parents). In each occasion of confession, it was our task to discover the real reasons behind each fornication. Most often in a woman who cannot be moral, there is lack of a father's expressed love and a consequent lack of love and respectful care for her own being. She believes she is worthless anyway, so why not be the tool of any man who comes along? Especially since to be touched seems to reach such vacant and needy places deep inside.

Having a pastor or close friend merely tell you that you are forgiven and released from the sin of fornication most likely will not completely set you free. You should, again with the help of a prayer minister or Christian counselor, talk about and pray through all the hidden (and not-so-hidden) childhood wounds and resentments. A love and respect for your own person may also have to be resurrected. Seeing the causes of fornication must not be allowed as an excuse for sin but as root rottenness producing sin in the present. When you recognize root causes and understand that the real reasons for promiscuity were not first sexual but psychological, that can help you to cease viewing all sexual impulses as nasty. It will enable you to allow true and proper human impulses to flow in sexual areas. With the help of a qualified Christian counselor or a prayer minister, you can develop a new sexual identity that will be cherished rather than feared.

Any complete sexual act, whether fornication, adultery, homosexuality, or some other aberration, unites your spirit with the other. "Or do you not know that the one who joins himself to a harlot [or any other illicit partner] is one body with her? For He says, 'The two will become one flesh'" (1 Cor. 6:16). God has so built our spirits that whatever woman a man enters, their spirits are united to each other from that moment on. Each person's spirit seeks, from the moment of union, to find, fulfill, nurture, and cherish the one who entered into that union with him/her.

If a flower is planted in good soil, it sends out roots and blooms where it is planted. It cannot bloom and produce properly or fully in alien, arid soil. In exactly the same way, God has designed us to be planted by marriage ceremony and subsequent sexual union in the fertile soil of our own spouse's body, heart, mind, soul, and spirit. We cannot come to fullness of life in any other soil. Only Paula is good soil for me. Only Paula can tell me who I am as a man. Any other woman, however comely of face, figure, or character, must tell me a lie that confuses. For that reason the Bible says, "But whoso committeth adultery with a woman lacketh understanding: he that doeth it *destroyeth his own soul*" (Prov. 6:32, KJV, emphasis added).

Unfortunately, however, once a wrong union has been entered, our spirit still remembers that union and seeks to fulfill the other. If there have been many immoral unions with many partners, our spirit becomes like an overloaded transformer, trying to send its current in too many directions. Having been delivered by confession, absolution, and prayer for separation of their spirit from their illicit partners, people who have been ministered to have often cried out, "I have never felt so free. I didn't realize how scattered I felt. I feel together again." Of course! Their spirits were no longer having to search heaven and earth to find and fulfill dozens of forgotten partners!

If you have chosen to walk through the healing process with the help of a prayer minister or Christian counselor, please understand the fullness of the task. As you confess the sin of sexual immorality, you will not only be forgiven by the authority in Jesus, not only be encouraged to seek out and forgive roots, not only have malformed structures transformed, but by the power of God in the name of Jesus you will also be separated from the spirit of the person involved in the immoral act with you. You will be able to forget that union (or unions). You will be loosed from that one (or those people). Your spirit will be set free to cleave only to your own husband (or wife). For the Word of God declares that what is loosed on the earth is loosed in heaven.

Adultery

Some of the same causes that lead us into fornication also lead us into adultery. Adultery is sexual union with a person other than one's own spouse. If a married person has intercourse with an unmarried person, the first commits adultery, the other fornication.

Because present troubles in some marriages are obviously creating vulnerability and driving us to seek illicit relationships, sometimes it may not appear that childhood roots affect those of us who commit adultery. We may protest sincerely that were it not for the present untenable circumstances in our marriage, there would be no difficulty in remaining faithful.

This may be true in part, for we cannot ignore present causes. However, with the help of your prayer minister or Christian counselor, deeper, more powerful causes for infidelity need to be searched for mainly in childhood roots. Roots of bitterness, often hidden and unconscious, determine largely how we receive and react to present stimuli to our conscious awareness. Because such roots are often unseen, they have more power to drive us beyond our control when present circumstances pressure us.

For example, the most common present cause Paula and I have seen is failure of one or both partners to communicate. The result is loneliness and vulnerability. Any person in such circumstances is dying emotionally inside, whether aware of it or not. Sooner or later someone comes along who is able to penetrate behind barriers to communicate heart to heart and soul to soul. It feels so wonderful to come alive again emotionally that the person cannot feel guilty as sexual desires begin to awaken. He or she finds that bewildering, having expected great warning signals or feelings of heavy guilt. A man, for instance, may be unaware that because his spirit is so dead it will not send any signals of conscience. His coming alive again emotionally in his soul's faculties can feel so good that he can't believe the relationship is wrong or sinful. If he continues and enters into adultery, he may find his mind weakly reminding him of God's laws, but his heart is singing. He thinks he is "in love." Now he is thoroughly confused. Can God's laws be wrong? Can they be only men's imaginations? Surely he wouldn't feel so alive if this were sin. He does not know that if he divorced his wife and married this "soul mate," she would soon be identified as a "mother" and thereby also become one not to be shared with, and he would soon have to find another "soul mate."

Nevertheless, no matter how compelling the present loneliness or how confusing the seeming happiness in the sinful relationship and its accompanying lack of guilt, behind all of these things may lie resentment regarding a poor relation with his mother or some other bitter root. That bad root is the real cause, activated by present problems.

This pattern appears with many variations—the secretary, a partner at work, a best friend's husband or wife, someone who counsels another or who receives counsel, the next-door neighbor, someone in the family such as a brother- or sister-in-law, someone who works on the same committee in some good work, and so on. Some people go out specifically seeking adulterous relationships. Such people are to be pitied. But most often normally "good" people are blinded by some hidden needs or broken areas until proximity to just the "right-wrong" person develops. We need the help of a prayer minister to discover what was actually operating in adulterous relationships and deal with causes, not merely results.

OTHER ABERRANT FORMS OF SEXUALITY

The Scriptures are clear and adamant concerning all aberrational forms of sex. By aberrational forms we mean incest, mating with animals, *ménage à trois* (three in one bed), homosexuality, and the like.

If there is a man who commits adultery with another man's wife, one who commits adultery with his friend's wife, the adulterer and the adulteress shall surely be put to death. If there is a man who lies with his father's wife, he has uncovered his father's nakedness; both of them shall surely be put to death, their bloodguiltiness is upon them. If there is a man who lies with his daughter-in-law, both of them shall surely be put to death; they have committed incest, their bloodguiltiness is upon them. If there is a man who lies with a male as those who lie with a woman, both of them have committed a detestable act; they shall surely be put to death. Their bloodguiltiness is upon them. If there is a man who marries a woman and her mother, it is immorality; both he and they shall be burned with fire, that there may be no immorality in your midst. If there is a man who lies with an animal, he shall surely be put to death; you shall also kill the animal. If there is a woman who approaches any animal to mate with it, you shall kill the woman and the animal; they shall surely be put to death. Their bloodguiltiness is upon them.

If there is a man who takes his sister, his father's daughter or his mother's daughter, so that he sees her nakedness and she sees his nakedness, it is a disgrace; and they shall be cut off in the sight of the sons of their people. He has uncovered his sister's nakedness; he bears his guilt. If there is a man who lies with a menstruous woman and uncovers her nakedness, he has laid bare her flow, and she has exposed the flow of her blood; thus both of them shall be cut off from among their people. You shall also not uncover the nakedness of your mother's sister or of your father's sister, for such a one has made naked his blood relative; they shall bear their guilt. If there is a man who lies with his uncle's wife he has uncovered his uncle's nakedness; they shall bear their sin. They shall die childless. If there is a man who takes his brother's wife, it is abhorrent; he has uncovered his brother's nakedness. They shall be childless.

—Leviticus 20:10–21

Homosexuality will be spoken of more fully in the next chapter. Here we discuss other sexual strongholds. At the time we wrote *Healing the Wounded Spirit*, we found statistics that reported one in five women had been molested. Since that writing, many surveys put the rate at one in every three, and increasing.[1] As the nation turns from God and His Word, we are given over "to degrading passions" (Rom. 1:26).

Incest and molestation

When a father or stepfather molests or lies with his daughter, the greatest possible harm is done not only to her but also to himself. He is confused, shamed, and destroyed, whether or not he is aware of loss. His very manhood has been degraded. He has shattered the essence of what it is to be a father, as one who is to protect the women in his care and who is to nurture his daughter's sexuality in holiness. She has been destroyed. The essential capacity of her spirit to become a wife sexually, to entrust the holiness of her spirit through her body to a husband, has been shattered and defiled at its source. Her spirit's loyalty to honor her father has become confused and desecrated with the union of her spirit to his as a sexual partner. Her ability to relax and let her spirit refresh her husband in holy union is now dead. Only the grace of the Lord, not only to forgive, heal, and separate but also to re-create in her through His power to resurrect, can restore her as a wife and mother. After more than fifty years in prayer ministry, we have discovered nothing more destructive and defiling than incest!

Girls becoming women should feel free and secure to openly attract their fathers' wholesome adoration. The young girl and both parents should know her motives are innocent and allow it honorably. A father should be delighted with his daughter and should tell her so. But many men read "come on" signals and fail to comprehend, or their conscience is so weak they override its signals and respond bestially.

For this reason many girls who are molested or raped feel guilty. They often feel they have done something to bring it on. What a shame it is that her God-given power to allure a man properly has now become something nasty to her! She may be afraid to ever let her physical beauty shine again. If in anger or rebellion she goes the other way and flaunts her physical beauty to trap men sexually, such a woman is not truly confident, even if she wields great sexual power to seduce. She is afraid to let her real beauty live for dread of pain at deepest levels in which her spirit still recoils in shame and hurt from her father. Her heart and spirit may feel confused, craving forgiveness as though for real guilt for seducing him, but her mind should be released by comprehension of what really went on, which was not her fault.

Further, a girl taken by her own father or stepfather finds her relationship to her mother fractured as well. Should she tell her mother? What would that do to her mother's marital life? What will it do if she doesn't tell? That she has taken her mother's bed place causes ambivalent feelings of the flesh to run rampant. There can be, but are not always, some of the following emotions: unwanted glee and guilt that she has beaten her mother in the game of allurement; shame that she has defiled her mother's bed but unpreventable nasty delight if for any reason she needed to wound or punish her mother; strong feelings of matehood toward her father, perhaps as strongly self-rejected; great desire to share with Mama countered by fear that blocks; possible fear of pregnancy; perhaps virulent hatred or aversion to the father—for which she can make no reply when the mother says, "Why can't you be nice to your daddy?" or "What's the matter between you two lately?"

If you are a woman who suffered from childhood sexual abuse, no doubt Satan has deceived you into believing that you are different from any other girl you know. You may be thinking, "After all, how many women I know have managed to seduce their own fathers? I'm really just a disgusting person with no self-control. No one would like me or even want to be around me if they really knew." You need to discover that not only are you innocent, but also you are not alone. The best way for you to discover that is by sharing your experience, preferably with a prayer minister who can talk through your experience with you to the point of healing. On the other hand, be careful about sharing your story with some people. Often choosing to share with someone who does not have a proven track record of confidentiality will undo all the good accomplished by sharing with the right people.

One-time occurrences, or even several, are not as damaging as being forced to become a regular incestuous partner. In each of the many cases we have counseled, we have seen the same effect—a deadness of heart and eye concerning what it is to be a woman. It is as though such women have given up and know themselves to be nothing but tools to be used and discarded. If you have suffered such long-term abuse, it will be nearly impossible for you to find healing on your own. You need to put yourself in the care of a prayer minister who can lead you into healing. It will not happen quickly or easily, but the journey to wholeness can be finished. Much healing may have to be administered, and it will take the efforts of an experienced helper to avoid transference, confused emotions, and issues of dependency. Resurrecting another is not always as clean and clear as calling out, "Lazarus, come forth." We are not the Lord, though He acts through us; resurrection of another affects us—and we must guard our own hearts as we serve. More prayer ministers and counselors fail in this attempt than in any other, which is why it is so important to choose a highly recommended person to help you take your own journey to resurrection and wholeness.

Ménage à trois

Ménage à trois refers to two women in bed with one man, or two men with one woman. Behind *ménage à trois* is often a hunger to fill longings in the heart that could only be satisfied by true sexual blessedness. Some forms of lust occur when true hungers are prevented right satisfaction, causing that energy to seek false release (augmented by fleshly desire and satanic influence). When deadness of spirit prohibits true fulfillment and consequent hunger couples with other flaws in our characters, the answer for resultant lust can be identified by the mind in terms of some aberrational form such as *ménage à trois*. No aberrational experience truly satisfies, but it thrills enough to hold promise; thus it captivates and becomes compulsive. Once started down that path, the person must either tire or find more and more degradations to explore.

Sometimes *ménage à trois* happens as a throwback to excessive performance orientation. There is great hunger to experiment and greater lust to do something to defile, to destroy the good-guy image. One pastor we knew could not receive my warnings concerning performance orientation and his need to destroy his good-guy role. He wound up in *ménage à trois* and so frightened himself that he plunged back into performing with a vengeance. We wonder what will come next—unless grace intervenes.

Sometimes it is strict obedience to law that fuels fires that erupt into *ménage à trios*: "The strength of sin is the law" (1 Cor. 15:56, KJV). Here the motive power differs from performance orientation only in that the specific way of being righteous is by legal rigidity. That coerces repression, for the Pharisee must not let his feelings or thoughts even enter such fields. One wise old pastor said to me, "John, no man can keep the birds from flying over his head, but you don't have to let them nest in your hair." No one can keep lustful thoughts out of his mind or heart. But a man has not "committed adultery with her already in his heart" (Matt. 5:28) until he purposefully entertains such things in his imagination and dwells upon them. He has only to pray silently, "That's me, Lord, a normal sinner. Forgive me," and go on, forgetting what lies behind. But the rigid ones fight the slightest feelings and thoughts, trying desperately to maintain fleshly righteousness, and thereby doom themselves to endless struggles, until some explode into *ménage à trois* or some other form of degradation. Their obedience was for the wrong reason, not from a live spirit that rests in Jesus, but from the vainglory of a self-righteous heart and mind.

Pornography

Pornography has this same appeal—a no-no offered to a child needing to rebel. To those who have long ago cut free from parental taboos and found their own foundations in love, pornography is something rank and detestable, not something alluring. Getting the help of a prayer minister can break the hold of pornography by getting at roots of rebellion and resentment in childhood.

Whatever the aberration, a prayer minister will find out what is the unique causal factor in each case and so deal with roots. Taking these issues to a prayer minister will also grant you the needed accountability to find lasting victory over these snares.

As You Begin the Search for Help in Being Set Free From Sexual Sin...

You may be reading through this chapter and feel that you are bound to certain behaviors that are unforgivable, but there is no sin so great that God the Father cannot forgive through the Lord Jesus (except the sin against the Holy Spirit), however aberrant the sin may be. After all these years, I (John) sometimes have such feelings of anger and revulsion at a man who regularly sexually abuses his daughter that I am sure I must be a most unfit vessel to pronounce that man's forgiveness. But the work of mercy is the Lord's, not mine. (Nor is it your prayer minister's.) And so the prayer of forgiveness will always work wonders, no matter what I or any other prayer minister may feel. Just as Communion and baptism are valid, no matter what the spiritual condition of the celebrating priest, so you need not worry about your personal feelings about what you may be going through. Our yet-undealt-with angers cannot block the efficacy of confession, repentance, and forgiveness. A counselor or prayer minister in Christ is called to honor the office as a representative of Christ, not surrender to whatever wayward feelings assail his or her own heart.

You should also be aware that sometimes in receiving help with sexual issues, things can become needlessly confusing. You may find yourself struggling with feelings of lust toward your prayer minister, but be open with him or her, and by faith and experience he or she will be able to identify what that actually is. Having placed myself as a prayer minister daily in my Lord's hands, and placing the cross between the person to whom I minister and myself, I know Jesus keeps my heart. He will also keep the heart of your prayer minister to handle all of the feelings that may be stirred in your heart as you work out those things that are hidden in your past. Just as a true prayer minister will find his or her security first with the Lord and then with his or her own spouse, I also find my security in Paula's love, so that even if my sinful, lusty heart were itself stirred in reaction to a person's feelings, I would not entertain or act on such feelings. I know then that those strange feelings of lust are not my own, but the other's lust that the Holy Spirit enables me to feel; this is one way discernment can operate in me. A question or two usually discovers that to be true, and the feelings in me, having existed only to alert me to what the other is feeling, quickly depart.

This is an important lesson that needs to be learned. Too many have fallen into honoring "love" feelings as real and have succumbed to temptation.

Some teachers have insisted, some adamantly, that no man should ever minister to a woman and that no woman should minister to a man. Such advice seems wise, but it stems mainly from fear, not godly wisdom. As you begin to reach out for help with sexual issues, keep in mind that if you are a woman, you may need the ministry of a man to become whole. Jesus, of course, did not have the benefit of such teachers' wisdom or He would never have been caught ministering so long alone with the woman at the well (John 4)!

Some insist that a man should minister to a woman only if his wife or other witness is present. That is wise and preferable, but it is not always possible; it is helpful more because two are better than one (Eccles. 4:9) than for fear of sexual wrongdoing.

Let us not celebrate the strength of the flesh or of Satan and his hosts. If a Christian is not strong enough to be trusted in the arena with either a man or a woman, he ought not to be ministering, period. A man who lives alone, or who is presently in trouble with his wife, ought to protect himself whenever possible by having others with him. At the first signs of untoward involvement he should resign that ministry situation or refuse to continue unless others are present, so as never to give the flesh opportunity. The fact that some counselors have fallen must not be allowed to stampede us into wrong solutions. There are many risks in prayer ministry, but we do not answer them by worldly wisdom devoid of scriptural backing. The example of Jesus is disciplined freedom, not fear and retreat—or shall we insist that no male medical doctor examine a woman for fear of sex?

On the other hand, I have shared these warnings because I know of many prayer ministers who have become involved sexually with the people to whom they minister, especially when ministering in the area of sex. The two most serious pitfalls we have seen prayer ministers fall into are depression and sexual affairs with the persons to whom they minister. Those who fall sexually represent a very small fraction of all prayer ministers, but if it happens once, it happens too often. It can be prevented if it is understood that most often such affairs started because the prayer minister naïvely thought the feelings of attraction he felt were really his instead of simple empathetic identification. As you seek help, ask God to lead you to someone who is at one with his wife or her husband, as we have said. I have no hesitation to advise that the person who is not secure in his or her own marriage to stop until the heart is settled again.

MASTURBATION AND ORAL SEX

We cannot leave the field without discussing two other areas of great sexual concern in some people. Many come to us confessing an obsession with masturbation. We treat that condition quite oppositely from all the others we have described. Usually what has occurred is that a child, growing up in a tension-filled home, coming into puberty, learned that the experience of ejaculation (for a man) or climax (for a woman) brings a great feeling of release and peace. When the need for relief from tension is coupled with the power of a repressed no-no, masturbation often sets in as a habit. It becomes compulsive over the years by a process of fleshly struggle and continued identification with relief.

Scripture does not mention masturbation per se. It only mentions wet dreams and uncleanness (Lev. 15:16; Deut. 23:10) and the sin of Onan, who spilled his seed on the ground to avoid producing offspring for his deceased brother, whose wife he was bound by custom to marry (Gen. 38:9). The latter was not a case of masturbation, as some claim, but of interrupted intercourse.

Many take this silence about masturbation to mean it is not a sin. We disagree. We believe it is always sin, for it is an idolatrous expression of self-fulfillment, and idolatry is always forbidden by Scripture. But though in other circumstances I (John) often speak to make others feel guilty, knowing that as the route to the cross, here I act in the opposite way. This is the one time I will tell a person not to feel guilty (about the masturbation itself).

The true guilt concerns not sexuality first but idolatry. The person is using his body to find the comfort and release he should find in prayer to God. The same principle is true of inordinate smoking, drinking, golfing, fishing, or whatever we overuse to find the release we should have found in God directly through prayer. I explain to the person about identification of masturbation with relief and the power of repression and the guilt of idolatry, and then I say, "Let's find forgiveness for that idolatry and see if we can take some of the steam out of this habit by not struggling with it so hard." I may add, "If you slip, OK, forgive yourself. But struggling with it as a no-no only increases tension and gives it added power." (Note, I never counsel the same way for any other sin, such as adultery. That simply must be stopped, whatever the cost.) This particular habit has built-in channels inside the body—reflexes that are best defeated by ignoring them rather than frontally attacking them.

The same principle was involved when I as a youth had developed a habit of cursing. When I decided to stop, the battle was on. I discovered then that the more energy I poured into the struggle, the more fuel somehow went to the habit. But when I turned to Jesus and put my eyes on Him and ignored the battle, trusting His forgiveness for each slip, the battle was soon over. Fleshly struggle adds power to the problem. Rest in Jesus defuses it.

When fantasy is involved (and with masturbation it almost always is), the issue becomes morally weightier than that of inordinate smoking, drinking, or golfing. For Jesus equated sexual fantasizing with adultery: "Anyone who looks at a woman lustfully has already committed adultery with her in his heart" (Matt. 5:28, NIV). Yet we have found that even in this case, heaping guilt will only serve to strengthen the tendency to sin. For if someone tells you not to picture a red polka-dotted monkey, what will your mind immediately picture? Likewise, if someone thunders at you to stop picturing sexual images, that has virtually created a track for your thoughts to run on.

So I teach the person that the moment the temptation to fantasize or stimulate oneself arises, to recognize it but not to be fearfully concerned; just turn the eyes of the mind to Jesus and find someone to pray for in order to distract the train of the impulse from its track. In prayer I say, "In the name of Jesus I forgive each instance of masturbation, and now I speak directly to the body, loosing it from this habit. I break this identification of peace and emotional release with masturbation and say to the inner being that it is to find release now in prayer at the foot of the cross, not in physical stimulation." Many have returned to say, "What do you know, John, it worked! I don't have to struggle with it anymore." Some add, "Once in a while I still slip, but it isn't a compulsion anymore. I forgive myself and don't get caught up in self-condemnation."

I plead with prayer ministers not to treat masturbation as a demon to be exorcised and not to come down harshly on the person. Masturbation is simply a bomb in the flesh we want quietly to defuse.

The second great concern many have is about oral sex. Again, I have found no direct discussion in the Scriptures. It may be there, but to date I have not found it. The Word does say, "That each of you know how to possess his own vessel in sanctification and honor" (1 Thess. 4:4). That is the key I follow: whatever honors the other. A second principle is, whatever seems natural, the way God designed things to be, is OK. Oral sex does not seem natural to me. The tongue is made for food and speech. Genitals are built for genitals. I might add that until recently, the vast majority of

Christians have always rejected this practice. Where Scripture is silent, the collective discernment of the body of Christ should be considered.

A number have come to me saying, "But my wife wants it, and oral sex seems to be the only way she can become aroused enough to enjoy intercourse." Often a wife complains that her husband demands oral sex or that his sexual needs are excessive. Frequently the cause here is simply that he feels her withholding a part of her inner self from him (though she may be quite willing to go through all the physical expressions of love). Because he never feels "met" and cannot identify what is missing, he is compelled to ask for more and more, and the "more" never satisfies, for the sharing is experienced through walls.

A long time ago the Lord clearly, but not audibly, said to me, "John, fight the warfare with whatever level of faith and whatever weapons you have. What you can do in innocence today may not be appropriate to tomorrow's need or level of faith." Therefore my counsel to such people has been that the real reasons they cannot be aroused are probably psychological. Look at the roots. Meanwhile it may or may not be sin, but do what you have to do to keep the relationship from failing. I may change that counsel as the Lord reveals His Word more clearly and gives me more wisdom. To be clearer, I do believe that a regular practice of oral sex would be much less than God intends, perhaps sinful. We do not do this ourselves, because we meet spirit to spirit and heart to heart, and such means of arousal are not needful for us. Again, there should be no need to put a heavy guilt trip on yourself if you are a married couple who finds oral sex pleasurable. (We speak only of some oral stimulation for arousal, not the use of it rather than normal sex; we would simply say to stop that practice.)

Many have written to us, having heard us speak on this subject, wanting us to speak out more forcibly condemning oral sex. We need to make clear that even if our predilection were to do so and though our own practice is to avoid oral sex, as prophets and teachers of the Lord, we can only speak out forcibly (as we have about adultery) where the Word of God is unequivocal, either by direct statement or by inference. Prophets and teachers must be careful as St. Paul was in 1 Corinthians 7, to distinguish when the Lord was speaking (v. 10), when Paul spoke but thought himself trustworthy (v. 25), or when what he said was his own opinion (vv. 12, 40). We plead with well-meaning Christians not to let their zeal cause men to twist God's Word to say what it doesn't say, nor to push or condemn God's servants for not taking stands in areas of controversy in which the Word of God is not unmistakably decisive. We cannot make a definitive statement when God's Word (to our knowledge) does not, no matter how much we might want to.

DATING AND MAKING OUT

Finally, concerning dating and "making out" (which today means what petting, sparking, or spooning meant to other generations). The question asked so often is, "How far can I go before it is sin?" This question (and all the dating difficulties young people find themselves involved in today) arises because our culture is distinctly unbiblical. There was no dating in Bible lands. Therefore the Bible does not lay down direct guidelines. There was no need then. The Song of Solomon does say, "I adjure you, O daughters of Jerusalem, by the gazelles or by the hinds of the field, that you will not arouse or awaken my love, until she pleases" (Song of Sol. 2:7).

Today's children have been freed from the docetic mind-set of previous centuries that taught some people to think sex was nasty (see chapters 9–11 of *The Elijah Task*) and that had caused them to fear all bodily emotions and passions. That freedom is good. They also have been delivered from inhibitions of touch and sight that were born of prudery rather than respect for the holiness of a person. That also we view as good. However, today's culture is much too devoid of the sense of the holy and of proper respect for modesty. Moral laws have been scoffed at and scrapped by most of the culture. Therefore young people have few of the safeguards in dating that we older ones felt compelled to observe. Add to that today's relaxed views of chaperoning and the mobility available to young people, and parents are reduced to nothing but bare trust in God and prayer. The culture also teaches the opposite of Christian love—to get what you want with no respect for others. Christian girls are now often disrespected and rejected if they won't put out. It is a frightening time for parents of teenage young people and for unmarried people.

The teenage years are too late for basic teachings. By then we reap what was sown or not sown in childhood. A child well coached during the preteen years, whose parents' lives exemplify what they say, is well armed for entrance into teenage dating dilemmas. We have known girls who walked home many miles in the night or chose the path of loneliness during high school years to keep themselves for the Lord and for their husbands-to-be. Praise God for their testimony and for their parents' solid teachings and example.

Some kissing may be all right for young people. But I (John) could not bring myself to kiss a girl unless I had known her a long time. To me a kiss meant more than physical touch; it involved meeting and cherishing. I could not kiss a girl apart from meaning, just for the "thrill" of it. That was a travesty to me; it meant to my heart the same kind of dishonesty as to come into the house of God and go through the motions of worship without meaning it. I only went with two others before Paula, and I was quite serious about each. I watched Paula several weeks before asking her for a date, and then I did not ask to kiss her until we had dated several weeks. Loren had the same kind of approach to dating. And Mark, John, Tim, and Andrea thought in like manner. Morality is ingrained; it is "caught" from one's parents.

Although you may be able to go so far and stop, we admonish you with this warning: what you can do today may not be what you will be able to continue to do and still be able to stop as your relationship grows. So there is no hard-and-fast rule for what you can do without it being too much. During certain times of the month, desire is greater and resistance lower. Certainly, all genital areas should be off limits before marriage. The breasts should be reserved for the husband only. (See Proverbs 5:18–19, and especially verse 20: "For why should you, my son, be exhilarated with an adulteress, and embrace the bosom of a foreigner?") How can a young man know whether this one whose bosom he desires to embrace will be his or another's wife? Even if he is sure a girl will become his wife, premarital petting of the breasts is forbidden by Scripture. (See Ezekiel 23:3, 8, 21.) Our counsel to you as you become more serious in your premarital relationship is that you not give yourself the opportunity by being alone together too much. Double-date and go to parties together. Flesh cannot be trusted once increasing trust opens doors. Not love but flesh will push you to go too far.

Again, this may not be so much about accepting forgiveness for overstepping bounds as it is about uncovering childhood flaws that create vulnerability. Most often, unfortunately, we do not have opportunity for preventive medicine, but let us hope that these few words may help to prevent you from ruining the gift God has given you for one only. Every year (we have now been married fifty-six years) Paula and I rejoice in the Lord more and more that by His grace He has kept us all of our lives only for each other.

We have brought up many things that may cause you embarrassment, shame, or guilt, but please be sure that there is no sin so great that God the Father cannot forgive through the Lord Jesus (save that against the Holy Spirit), however abhorrent the sin, and no wound that the blood of Jesus can't heal. The work of mercy and grace is the Lord's, not mine, and so if you are one who has committed any of these acts, or if you are someone who needs healing in any of these areas, the prayer for forgiveness always works wonders, no matter what amount of guilt or shame you may feel. So you need not worry. Any yet-undealt-with roots of bitterness, anger, judgments, or guilt cannot block the efficacy of confession, repentance, and forgiveness. The Bible says in 1 John 1:9, "If we confess our sins, He is faithful and righteous to forgive us our sins and to cleanse us from all unrighteousness." This is a promise from our Lord that we can accept through faith.

CHAPTER 7

HEALING GENDER IDENTITY ISSUES

And God created man in His own image, in the image of God He created him; male and female He created them. And God blessed them; and God said to them, "Be fruitful and multiply, and fill the earth, and subdue it."
—GENESIS 1:27–28

Professing to be wise, they became fools, and exchanged the glory of the incorruptible God for an image in the form of corruptible man and of birds and four-footed animals and crawling creatures. Therefore God gave them over in the lusts of their hearts to impurity, that their bodies might be dishonored among them. For they exchanged the truth of God for a lie, and worshiped and served the creature rather than the Creator, who is blessed forever. Amen. For this reason God gave them over to degrading passions; for their women exchanged the natural function for that which is unnatural, and in the same way also the men abandoned the natural

function of the woman and burned in their desire toward
one another, men with men committing indecent acts
and receiving in their own persons the due penalty of
their error.

—ROMANS 1:22–27

Before we discuss how to let go of gender identity issues,
it is important to know how they root themselves in the
individual. It is important to discover the person's early
life with his or her parents. In all our years of prayer ministry,
we have never found a person who had healthy relationships
with either one or both parents to have any issues with gender
identity—except when the gender identity problems come from
rape or molestation. In this chapter we will deal with gender identity issues as a result of rape or molestation, and in the forms of
homosexuality, of feeling as if one were born the wrong sex or
what we call "mistaken identity." It is important that we deal with
this gender identity issue because it is another product of the past.
Our Lord did not originally create us to have confusion or hurts
based on the gender that we were born. He created us male and
female and is pleased with His creation (Gen. 1:31). He wants us
to be free to be all that He made us to be; therefore, healing the
rejection and hurt as they relate to our gender is part of letting
go of our pasts and grasping the freedom He purchased for our
future by way of the cross.

RAPE AND MOLESTATION

Song of Solomon 8:4 says, "Do not arouse or awaken love until it so desires" (NIV). There is a right time for sexual desires to be awakened. Rape or molestation stimulates before that time and is very damaging to a child. It can tempt a child to reject his or her own sexual feelings as something dirty and violent. In reaction, a victim may vow not to feel "evil" sexual feelings. That inner vow can only shut off good impulses, but not sinful ones, for fleshly striving cannot stop evil. Prevented from flowing in God-given channels, sexuality then finds other expressions. Rape can also tempt a victim to reject his or her own gender. A girl who is molested can blame the rape on the fact that she is female. A boy who is raped may recoil in disgust at sharing the same gender as the rapist.

I (John) knew a youth who was molested by an older man. That young person eventually married and had children. But that early association so worked on him that when the marriage became difficult, as happens to most everyone until issues are worked through, he divorced his wife and fled from "too troubling encounters" in relationship to the opposite sex into the "safer" embrace of a male lover. It would not be that he would have found a homosexual relationship to be "safe," but his fleshly striving and rejection of his own gender chased him into it because he had not been properly healed and loosed from the pain and memory of that first unwanted encounter. Eventually he contracted HIV and wound up in a home for homosexuals who were dying from AIDS. Weeks before his death, several young people and I visited with him. He was able to receive the Lord Jesus as his Savior, and he went home to heaven. From this man's misguided life and death, and from many other experiences in ministering to homosexuals, I saw the devastating effects of molestation, particularly how it so often seduces men into a homosexual lifestyle.

HOMOSEXUALITY

Homosexuality is not a thing by itself. It possessed culture and history long before Sodom and Gomorrah. Other aberrations do not claim to be a valid style of life, but homosexuality wraps about itself rationalizations, defenses, veneers, postures, and a way of living that sometimes even claims to be Christian. In order for you to be free of this entanglement, it is important to see its roots and to see its deceptions brought to light by the truth of God's Word. The apostle Jude wrote, "Dear friends, although I was very eager to write to you about the salvation we share, I felt I had to write and urge you to contend for the faith that was once for all entrusted to the saints. For certain men* whose condemnation was written about long ago have secretly slipped in among you. They are godless men, *who change the grace of our God into a license for immorality* and deny Jesus Christ our only Sovereign and Lord" (Jude 3–4, NIV, emphasis added).

Today some human rights groups appeal for acceptance of homosexuality as normal, God given, and healthy; they say that no one can survive as a Christian without a generous, loving, and accepting nature. But the Word of God is absolutely clear concerning homosexuality. It says that homosexuality is a sin, and our kindness to each other is not achieved by lessening the effects of disobeying God's law. His law is nothing but kindness toward

---

* Many biblical scholars believe "certain men" refers distinctly to homosexuals; the point is clear, whether this is the case or not.

us, and it was given purely for our benefit. We think to change or improve upon His law only to invoke the silliness of our fleshly reasonings, but the Word of God allows no other statement. See the following verses:

> If there is a man who lies with a male as those who lie with a woman, both of them have committed a detestable act; they shall surely be put to death. Their bloodguiltiness is upon them.
>
> —LEVITICUS 20:13

> You shall not lie with a male as one lies with a female; it is an abomination.
>
> —LEVITICUS 18:22

> For even though they knew God, they did not honor Him as God, or give thanks; but they became futile in their speculations, and their foolish heart was darkened. Professing to be wise, they became fools, and exchanged the glory of the incorruptible God for an image in the form of corruptible man and of birds and four-footed animals and crawling creatures. Therefore God gave them over in the lusts of their hearts to impurity, that their bodies might be dishonored among them. For they exchanged the truth of God for a lie, and worshiped and served the creature rather than the Creator, who is blessed forever. Amen. For this reason God gave them over to degrading passions; for their women exchanged the natural function for that which is unnatural, and in the same way also the men abandoned the natural function of the woman and burned in their desire toward one another, men with men committing indecent acts and receiving in their own persons the due penalty of their error.
>
> —ROMANS 1:21–27

Or do you not know that the unrighteous shall not inherit the kingdom of God? Do not be deceived; neither fornicators, nor idolators, nor adulterers, *nor effeminate [i.e. "effeminate, by perversion"], nor homosexuals,* nor thieves, nor covetous, nor drunkards, nor revilers, nor swindlers, shall inherit the kingdom of God.

—1 CORINTHIANS 6:9–10, EMPHASIS ADDED

Realizing the fact that law is not made for a righteous man, but for those who are lawless and rebellious, for the ungodly and sinners, for the unholy and profane, for those who kill their fathers or mothers, for murderers and immoral men *and homosexuals* and kidnappers and liars and perjurers, and whatever else is contrary to sound teaching.

—1 TIMOTHY 1:9–10, EMPHASIS ADDED

But for the cowardly and unbelieving and abominable [remember that Leviticus 18:22 calls homosexual activity an "abomination"] and murderers and immoral persons and sorcerers and idolaters and all liars, their part will be in the lake that burns with fire and brimstone, which is the second death.

—REVELATIONS 21:8

The only change from the Old Testament to the New Testament concerning homosexuality has to do with treatment. In the Old Testament the sole answer was death, whether from stoning by Israel or fire from heaven upon Sodom and Gomorrah. Today the answer is still the same—death. But Jesus has become that death for us, so the answer is, "Brethren, even if a man is caught in any trespass, you who are spiritual, restore such a one in a spirit of gentleness" (Gal. 6:1). The Christian answer is forgiveness and death on the cross, thus redemption from sin, whenever we will allow that to take place. It is to that end we write. Our hope is to place in people's minds and hearts tools for being delivered from homosexuality and other gender identity issues. Homosexuality is not an irreversible trap. We have seen a great many homosexuals delivered once and for all.

Our role as Christians for all people is to love the person, to hate that which destroys the life of Christ in him, and to assist as the Lord sets him free to become who he is meant to be in Christ. That task for homosexual individuals is made most difficult by the stance of the "gay community." Gay society acts to pull back "by fleshly desires, by sensuality, those who barely escape from the ones who live in error" (2 Pet. 2:18). The gay community takes a stance that anyone ought to see that their lifestyle is normal. (This is based on the Hitlerian maxim that a big enough lie will be accepted as truth.) Whoever doesn't agree to that lie is of course judgmental and filled with hate. This type of socialization makes those who are struggling with homosexuality even more confused because their first desire, like that of anyone else, is to be loved and accepted.

A gay person may agree with a prayer minister in grieving for parents and children in child abuse cases, or in the deliverance of an alcoholic, or in setting free someone who is psychotically paranoid. Both the homosexual and heterosexual can find common ground in recognizing, even biblically, the undesirability of such conditions. Normally, neither gay nor "straight" would have difficulty in concurring that the command, "Thou shalt not steal," is to be obeyed and that mercy is to be applied to a thief according to Galatians 6:1. Gays may celebrate the compassion of a prayer minister relative to everyone and everything else, but if that same prayer minister moves to set a brother free from homosexuality, suddenly the prayer minister is apt to be named a bigot who is judgmental and hateful—someone to be discredited and avoided.

But as the Word of God says in 2 Corinthians 4:2, "We do not use deception, nor do we distort the word of God" (NIV). We understand the power of the truth. We write, therefore, to heal those who are hurting and give guidance on how to set free those who desire deliverance. We do not desire to please, convince, or even give any credibility or acknowledgment to the gay agenda. There is no middle ground. Kindness and liberality happen by the grace of Christ for all sinners, not by relaxing one of the least of His commandments. We want to be up front with the truth of God's Word and minister the grace and redemption He has given to all of us through His death and resurrection on the cross.

We want to help heal this area in people's lives by looking at some situations that may have occurred in the past and identify ways that one can begin to overcome these issues. There are many ways homosexuality can root itself in an individual. Let's take a look at these now.

CAUSES FOR HOMOSEXUALITY

As the story at the beginning of this chapter indicates, when arousal is perpetrated by the wrong gender and expressions of "love" (it's not really love but poses as it) come from a homosexual source, a person can be triggered to become similarly oriented in adulthood, which leads to the gender identity issue of homosexuality. Rape can also predispose a person toward homosexuality. However, the main reason why people become homosexuals is failure to identify with the same-sex parent. In today's society many fathers no longer know how to be fathers, and mothers, increasingly, no longer know how to be mothers.

Before the Industrial Revolution (circa 1840), people lived in an agrarian and shop society. As soon as children could walk, especially boys, they accompanied their fathers either in the family fields or the workshop, which was usually in the home or attached to it. Fathers knew their task was to teach their children both their work skills and their ethics and morals. The command to teach children is strongly repeated many times in God's Word, Deuteronomy 6:7 being the most notable. That many fathers did teach their children is documented in the first verses of the first seven chapters of the Book of Proverbs. I quote only the first four verses of chapter 4:

> Hear, O sons, the instruction of a father, and give attention that you may gain understanding, for I give you sound teaching; do not abandon my instruction. *When I was a son to my father*, tender and the only son in the sight of my mother, *then he taught me* and said to me, "Let your heart hold fast my words; keep my commandments and live."
> —PROVERBS 4:1–4, EMPHASIS ADDED

Fathers were with their sons all day, working with them. They had opportunity to know their hearts; therefore, they were positioned to know their con games. Discipline was thus apt to be appropriate. Sons received admonition and, more importantly, nurture more regularly than they do now (Eph. 6:4).

Girls received the same from their mothers as they worked alongside, learning household skills and the morals of their faith.

But when the Industrial Revolution occurred, for the first time, fathers worked away from home. They were not with their children all day and consequently did not know their deceits. Scripture says, "Foolishness is bound up in the heart of a child; the rod of discipline will remove it far from him" (Prov. 22:15). Fathers now found it difficult to discipline appropriately. Some became too harsh, others too weak, and some abandoned their responsibility altogether.

Before World War I, the nuclear family—father, mother, and children—was surrounded by the extended family. When World War I came and fathers were gone from the home, grandfathers, uncles, older brothers, cousins, and others were there to give affection, nurture, and discipline. When the fathers returned, many were too wounded emotionally to give needful nurture. A generation did not receive proper fathering and, consequently, did not know how to father.

Then mobility happened. Many nuclear families moved away from the extended family. This meant that when World War II came, both the fathers and many mothers were gone from the home, so there were too few primary members to give nurture and discipline. An entire generation did not receive primary nurture.

When the fathers returned, again many were too wounded to do proper fathering. Behind in schooling and job opportunities, they would get Mama pregnant and go off to school and work, leaving the mother to raise the children. Another entire generation did not receive proper fathering. When that generation came of age, they could not give what they had not received; they did not know how to father.

The result of twentieth-century history has been the destruction of first the role of fathers and later of mothers. Inside every child is a great hunger for a father's love. When the need for love rises and a man fails to recognize what it is he really desires, he may not locate it where it belongs. Therefore, he may not seek reconciliation (if needed) and affection from his father; he may have no awareness that his father's love is what his heart is really seeking. *That hunger for his father's touch then easily translates into sexual touches and expressions of love from any man.* We have ministered to many homosexuals. We have never found one who experienced a good, loving relationship with his father. *Lack of fathering is perhaps the greatest present cause of the rapid growth of homosexuality in our day.*

When fathers are harsh, absent, or passive, some boys (especially the more sensitive) find their identity in their mothers. This exacerbates the lack of male identity. If a mother is critical or smothering, her son's aversion to females can deepen, as he puts up protective shields.

The same is true of lesbianism. Through appropriate touch and affection, a father keeps his daughter's heart alive to the need for male companionship. But like boys, girls also need to identify with the same-sex parent. What happened to fatherhood a few generations ago is now happening to motherhood. Feminism, divorce, single parenthood, and the resultant need to work away from home are leaving generations of mothers incapable of bonding with and training girls. Girls too are losing the sense of who they are.

Another common reason that people are led into homosexuality also has to do with fathers. When macho fathers have sensitive sons, they often don't know how to relate. That kind of father may be embarrassed by his son's more gentle, and possibly effeminate, ways. He may treat his son so insensitively or harshly, or with rejection, that the son retreats from his own masculinity into the female side of his nature. Or a father has such vices or unbecoming ways that his son can't accept that model of manhood and consequently rejects his own maleness. Even a strong athletic son may excel in sports while inwardly rejecting his own manhood. This rejection of manhood by rejecting their father's ways is a major reason why so many athletes become "gay"—a horrible misnomer. We have never ministered to anyone more miserable than homosexuals, though they may be unaware of it, while putting on a "gay" front.

In the same way, when delicate, demure mothers have strong daughters, they often do not know how to relate. A girl with strong leadership and aggressive qualities needs a mom to walk alongside and support her with undergirding strength. When her mother seems weak, conflicting, or morally undesirable, such a girl can feel tempted to reject her femininity.

That is not to say that all homosexual men are sensitive and all lesbians are strong women. Even a child who is very much like his same-sex parent can feel a lack of affinity with that parent if he feels estranged and can still suffer from a sense of being "other than."

With both homosexual boys and girls, the perceived contrast between themselves and peers increases the temptation to reject one's own gender. Many such boys and girls are mercilessly ridiculed for being different. Many sink into despair about ever being what they and others call "normal." What many don't realize is that they are normal. Proverbs 22:6 says, "Train up a child in the way he should go: and when he is old, he will not depart from it." This verse is not about imposing moral standards (although elsewhere, Scripture does call for that). Rather, the Hebrew conveys the sense that we should find the natural bent of the child and train him up to be who he was created to be.

God calls sensitive men to be sensitive. He calls strong women to be strong. He made them that way. When children falsely perceive that these qualities are out of step with their own gender, they can feel distanced from themselves. And that can set up a longing in boys to be more fully male or a longing in girls to be fully female. Not perceiving themselves to have those qualities, they can be tempted to fill the empty space inside themselves sexually, through others of their own gender.

BEING BORN THE "WRONG" SEX (OR "MISTAKEN IDENTITY")

Feeling like one was born the wrong sex or that he or she is living a mistaken identity also relates to prenatal wounding. Many to whom we have ministered perceived that they were the "wrong sex" for their parents' hopes and expectations. For example, parents who have three girls and become pregnant desperately hope for a boy, but it's another girl being formed in the womb. Or parents who have several boys now want a girl. We now know that in the mind of the spirit within us, even before the brain is fully formed, we know and react to many things. John the Baptist, six months along in his mother's womb, not only knew someone had come into his mother's presence, but also he knew it was Mary, the mother of our Lord. Further, though she was not even showing in her pregnancy, John knew she was pregnant and that the baby in her womb was his cousin, the Lord Jesus Christ! And he leaped for joy! (See Luke 1:41.)

We can't take time and space here to fully develop what is now known about prenatal knowledge and reactions inside the womb. (We recommend you read Dr. Verny's book *The Secret Life of the Unborn Child*[1] or learn from our other books in The Transformation Series, especially the chapters on healing the prenatal.) Suffice it to say here that children in the womb are aware of far more than we ever thought possible, and they react, in the mind of their spirits, even before the brain is formed or language is known. Pertinent to our subject, this is of great importance for several reasons.

One, boys who knew in the womb that their parents wanted a girl might become greatly confused. They may try to be their parents' girl. That in turn may create effeminacy. Identity becomes insecure, especially during their teenage years when identity is up for grabs because they are trying to find out who they are while trying to establish independence from their parents. Confusion lies at the root.

Two, this becomes exacerbated when macho fathers can't express acceptance and affirmation for sons who don't know why they have effeminate tendencies and feelings. Such sons are struggling to accept themselves and to overcome such yearnings in their nature. A father's affirmation, or lack of it, is crucial at those times. It often tips the scales to normalcy or aberrational expressions of sexuality. Our son Loren likes to exaggerate the teenage condition humorously by saying, "When kids hit the teenage years, the hormones turn on and the brains fall out!" We quote this to say that teen years and problems are normally difficult enough, but when prenatal woundings are part of the problem, that forms a powerful seduction to simply surrender to feeling like one is the wrong gender or even to homosexual feelings. Homosexuality, in such cases, actually has its origin not in actual homosexual sexual desires and feelings but in subliminal urges and feelings about identity from deep prenatal wounding.

As we mentioned at the beginning of this chapter, all of us have been created both male and female. Scripture says this when it states, "And God created man in His own image, in the image of God He created him; *male and female He created them*" (Gen. 1:27, emphasis added). The Word does not say that Adam was created male and Eve female, but that *they* were created male and female. God is a father, yet mothers are created in His image. Jesus is fully male, yet Eve was made in His image. God has within Him both male and female aspects. Since we are created in His image, the same is true of us. Otherwise, how could any man be part of the "bride" of Christ? We have both male and female poles within us. A man manifests mainly in the male pole of his being and seeks relationship with a wife, who alone can express the female side of him he can't fully manifest. Perhaps this can be taken as a *rhema* meaning behind Paul's statement that "he who loves his own wife loves himself" (Eph. 5:28), first because she is one with him. Loving her is thus loving himself. But perhaps also because her femininity expresses for him that part of himself he can't manifest, so loving her is actually a way of loving himself. Likewise a woman manifests in the female pole of her being and seeks a husband to express that half she can't.

The tragedy to which Paula and I have ministered countless times is that due to either prenatal wounding or early postnatal trauma, the male and female poles become crossed. When that happens, a man tries to manifest from within the female pole of his being and desperately seeks relationship with a man who can express for him his masculine side. Or a woman's poles become crossed and she seeks relationship with a woman to fulfill that missing part of her.

In marriage, this is one reason disappointment becomes so excruciating. When a partner's ways cannot be admired, when the maleness or femininity one so greatly needs to find expressed wonderfully is burlesqued or shamed, the pain can seem unbearable, which is one reason why so many want to bail out.

LETTING GO OF GENDER IDENTITY ISSUES

The Holy Spirit has given us keys to be set free from problems with gender and homosexuality. The idea that "once a homosexual always a homosexual" is Satan's lie. There is a more devastating lie: "I was created to be this way; this is who I was meant to be." Another horrible lie is that homosexuality is an acceptable alternate lifestyle. Another dispiriting lie is that homosexuality (or gender identity problems) can't be healed.

God creates no one to be homosexual or to be confused about who they are. Homosexuality is an abomination in the sight of God, as we saw in the scriptures listed earlier. God has given me great love for every homosexual, although I utterly abhor the sin that so devastates his life.

The Lord has given Paula and me several steps to help set free victims of rape and molestation, homosexuals, and those suffering with problems with gender identity. If you suffer from anything that we have mentioned in this chapter, and there are many more ways gender identity issues can manifest themselves (transgender, bisexuality, and the like), you must know that first, there is a mental battle that is more corporate than you, the individual. The corporate mental stronghold is as old as Sodom and Gomorrah. (A detailed discussion of a corporate mental stronghold is found in chapter 8 of *Why Good People Mess Up.*[2]) For the sake of brevity, a corporate mental stronghold is a way of thinking and reacting that has been built into society's culture. It takes on a life of its own and does not want to die. Its purpose is to take away rationality and freedom of thought and speech in order to take our minds captive in three ways:

1. Creating tunnel vision that blocks out truths that would otherwise set you free.

2. Manufacturing "buzzwords." Buzzwords are sayings that make no rational sense but are so emotionally laden that they are supposed to end all discussion. Typical buzzwords are: "I was born this way!" "It's an acceptable alternative lifestyle."

3. Entrapping not only minds but also the mentality of the entire populace so that we enact laws to protect rather than abolish the sin. It is not a hate crime to say that homosexuality is a sin.

Satan has worked overtime to sell these lies to make us captives to sin and bondage.

> If perhaps God may grant them repentance leading to the knowledge of the truth, and they may *come to their senses* and escape from the snares of the devil, having been *held captive by him to do his will.*
> —2 TIMOTHY 2:25–26, EMPHASES ADDED

> See to it that no one carries you off as spoil or *makes you yourselves captive by his so-called philosophy and intellectualism* and vain deceit (idle fancies and plain nonsense), following human tradition (men's ideas of the material rather than the spiritual world), just crude notions following the rudimentary and elemental teachings of the universe and disregarding [the teachings of] Christ (the Messiah).
> —COLOSSIANS 2:8, AMP, EMPHASIS ADDED

Anyone who desires to be free from homosexuality and issues of accepting their gender should find strong Christian friends, a prayer minister, or a Christian counselor who knows the truth as it is in God's Word to intercede and take captive the stronghold over the mind. A person will not be able to hear truth so long as the stronghold is uncontested and in place to hold in captivity. If that is you, perhaps the Holy Spirit is already working for you to have picked up this book, but even more you will know when the power of the stronghold is broken because you will begin to be able to hear. You will begin to see and offer insights you never could have seen before freedom began to arrive. You will no longer contest or offer buzzwords because the truth is setting you free from the corporate stronghold. Your countenance may actually begin to change as darkness begins to leave. Lightheartedness and joy will begin to emerge within you.

The next step is to share the details of your early and later life—fully and in the confidence of a trusted prayer minister or Christian counselor. Do not foreshorten inquiry into your history. Discuss openly as much as possible. If you can remember, share the details surrounding your prenatal history. If you are on good terms with your parents or relatives, find out more details to fill in missing or forgotten details. Allow the Holy Spirit to lead you to whatever wounds and coping mechanisms that may lie behind some of your choices.

After you and your prayer minister or Christian counselor have gathered a substantial history behind your choices, allow the work of inner healing to begin. Here are a couple stories (altered for confidentiality) to illustrate what is meant by "inner healing":

A man who came to me (John) had been born with a gentle, artistic nature. His father was not only macho but also harsh and judgmental, especially to this son whose ways became an affront to him. On the son's part, there was no way he could accept his father's model of manhood. He could not make himself follow that way. He thought it was a callous and thoughtless way of thinking and acting. Therefore, he fled to what he thought was the more humane but naturally effeminate side of his character. This offended his father all the more and widened the rift between them. Consequently, the son was left with a double bind. On the one hand, he desperately needed his father's love and approval. On the other hand, he vehemently rejected his father for his coarse ways. The hunger for his father's love soon seemed to be fulfilled by men of like temperament to his own and who gave him acceptance and expressions of approval. It was not long before such associations translated into sexual behaviors and then into full-blown homosexuality.

It would not have been successful merely to cast away the stronghold of homosexuality, to forgive sexual activities, and then pray, as will be explained later, to set his inner poles straight. Within him were bitter-root judgments of unforgiveness, that he would be rejected by other men the way his father had rejected him, and reactive patterns toward men in authority. Undealt with, these would soon have made any new lifestyle untenable. I led him to forgive his father from deep within, not merely superficially. He had tried many times to do that. What he needed was:

1. Authoritative pronouncement that his own sins of judging his father were forgiven.

2. Prayers that his habitual judgments and reactions to his father be reckoned as dead on the cross.

3. A new heart declared that could see the tenderness beneath the surface actions of seemingly insensitive, macho men.

We had to talk about such men until his eyes opened. Then his heart had to be healed by the Lord through my own acceptance of him, as a father who could see and appreciate and be proud of him for who God had created him to be. I affirmed his manhood as he expressed it in his own gentle way. Inner security in himself then replaced the need for the attention of men. When he was set free, he was able to maintain a heterosexual, normal lifestyle.

Another came who was his parents' fourth son. During pregnancy (there being, in those days, no way as we have today to determine gender before birth) his parents desperately wanted a daughter, but he was being formed as a boy. He felt in the womb that his parents' strong desire for a girl was tantamount to lack of acceptance and rejection of him as a boy. Unconsciously, he tried to be the daughter they wanted, adopting effeminate mannerisms. But he grew out of that, entered weight lifting, and became a strongly built young man. However, before he was ten years old, a man had taken advantage of his nature and molested him. Later on, others in the weight-lifting fellowship masturbated and drew him into group activities, which soon hooked into his unhealed prenatal wounds and led into homosexuality. He came across as so strong and masculine that few suspected or could conceive that he had now become distinctly homosexual. He came to me disgusted and wanting to be free.

I prayed first for the boy *in utero*, proclaiming, as though speaking for God, "I don't make mistakes. I didn't send you to be a woman; I sent you to be the strong man you have become. I lift the lie from your heart that you should have been female." I prayed about the molestation, separating his spirit from that union, washing him clean from the defilement by the water of the Lord. (As powerful as the blood of Jesus is, in this instance it may carry an association with certain sexual practices, for example, which makes it wiser to speak of His cleansing water.) I asked the Lord to bring to death on the cross the practiced tracks of the mind and heart that had been built in homosexual activities and to give him new reactions and responses to stimuli. In short, I simply asked for impartation of a wholesome heterosexual set of emotions and responses. Today, not only is he masculine in appearance, but also his heart beats in manly ways.

You can see through these stories that there are old ways in you that will have to die in order for the new to be resurrected. Forgiving yourself and those who hurt you as well as being accepted and perhaps reparented by a significant Christian brother or sister will play major roles in your being completely transformed. Since the time God gave us these steps, we have experienced much success in healing and transforming homosexuals and people with other gender identity problems. Although at times, change comes slowly. The only time it has failed completely is when the person had not yet come to hate his sin and did not want to truly be rid of it. An old true saying is, "You can't cast away a man's demon if he wants it."

Once the power of the stronghold has been broken, your biography has been discussed, and your inner being healed, then allow the Lord (as He leads you with a prayer minister or Christian counselor) to do what He told me to do with those to whom I have ministered on these issues. It is the one necessary, specific, and crucial key God has given us to complete this process. For this you should seek the help and guidance of a trained prayer minister or Christian counselor. Ask the Holy Spirit to help you see by vision the inner poles of masculinity and femininity. In my experience, they are like electrical anode and cathode poles, apart from each other but radiating to and through each other wholesomely. But in a homosexual or even merely effeminate person, the Lord shows me the poles bent toward each other and in some degree twisted around each other. In some, who have a lesser degree of confusion, the poles appear to be merely touching and bouncing off each other. In others, severely trapped, the poles look like intertwined vines, wrapping around each other like ivy encircling each other up a tree.

The Lord said to see Him reach in, take hold of the poles, and set them straight. Having seen that and prayed for it, I pray for all the feelings to flow normally, a man for a woman, a woman for a man. People have sometimes felt momentarily dizzy as we prayed that way. The head of a psychology department at a Christian college once told me what happened when a young homosexual man came to him for help. He said he didn't fully understand what I had taught but thought, "Why not try it?" So he ministered as I outlined above, and then with his faith choking back fear rising up in his throat, he asked the Lord to reveal to him what he needed to see to help this young man. Immediately, he saw the poles twisted as I had said. He asked the Lord to set the poles straight and celebrated seeing that happening by vision. He reported with great joy that the young man returned a week later to say that he had felt no more desires for a man and was feeling normal attractions to the women on campus.

Homosexuals and others with gender identity issues have arrested development. Before we are teenagers, our poles have not yet diverged into normal adult stance. It's as though they run together, and boys can't understand how anyone could be interested in a girl—*ugh*! Then the poles separate and radiate normally, and girls become "boy crazy" and boys find themselves "thinking about sex all the time," as one teenager complained to me.

I came to a church to minister, and I knew by the way the organist played that he was homosexual. He came for help. My helper and I ferreted out as many causes as we could discover in his childhood and prayed about those. We ministered inner healing. Then I took up authority and separated the poles, which truly had become twisted in his early life.

I returned to that church a year later, and the young man came to see my helper and me. One look and we could see that he was free! He was no longer homosexual at all. His entire countenance was different. Then he told us that one day early in the year after we prayed, he was in a doctor's office, and an attractive, well-built nurse came around the counter. He said, "I looked at her, and I went all googley inside. I couldn't stop staring at her." He had, at last in his thirties, become a normal teenager! Arrested development was now catching up.

Another young man, having recently received the same prayer and been set free from homosexual urges, said, "Is it normal to think about sex all the time?" In his mid-twenties, he had just become a young teenager emotionally. His poles finally were separating and acting normally—and gone were the yearnings for the touches of men.

A man came who had experienced fifty homosexual encounters in that one month previous! He was disgusted enough to be ripe for deliverance. I saw him one time and followed the steps outlined above. His poles looked like pretzels wound around each other. I prayed, seeing the Lord set his poles in order—remember, our God is not a God of confusion but of order. He left, and I never saw him again. Ten years later I received a letter from him. He wrote saying, "I'm still straight, and I have a lovely wife and two children." He wanted to thank me and to encourage me not to lose heart, to keep at it.

A final piece of advice: the defeated stronghold may not give up easily. The devil may counterattack, mainly through the corporate mental stronghold. It may be necessary to keep a "vigilante crew" at work for a while, preventing the return of the delusion and its aberrant behavior. The devil will try to come and lay an old feeling into your heart and old thoughts into your head. If you believe those old thoughts and feelings have real life and pick them up and act on them, the devil has made a major step in regaining his foothold. It is possible for this kind of thing to happen after you have been freed, but instead of believing they are real feelings and thoughts that have life, give them no life at all. In the Lord's authority, banish the feelings and thoughts, and if they persist, just ignore them. They are dead on the cross and have no real power. In a little while, the devil will tire of the game and go find someone else "he may devour" (1 Pet. 5:8, KJV).

In sum, being free from gender identity issues is not restricted as the province of a few adepts. Every Christian has authority and power in the Lord. Even if you feel overburdened with the guilt, shame, and isolation of this issue, you can be set free. But wisdom will inform you not to be a lone ranger. The Bible tells us that in a multitude of counselors there is victory (Prov. 11:14). Find a strong brother or sister in Christ to begin interceding for your freedom, and seek the help of a trained prayer minister or Christian counselor. Two are better than one (Eccles. 4:9). Wars are fought by armies, not individuals. Read John Paul Jackson's book *Needless Casualties of War*.[3] Don't let it frighten you away from the battle altogether. That wasn't John Paul's purpose. But heed his advice as you war against the stronghold and the principality who wields it corporately, armed with wisdom and humility. You *can* be set free. Homosexuality and other gender identity issues are not incurable. Take heart. You are more than a conqueror in Jesus.

CHAPTER 8

HE'S NOT HEAVY—
HE'S MY BROTHER

Bear one another's burdens, and thus fulfill the law of
Christ.

—GALATIANS 6:2

The subject of burden bearing is so important and needful
for the body of Christ to understand because it helps us as
we learn to let go of our pasts in two areas. First, burden
bearing is one of the primary ways that our Lord heals wounded
spirits. Second, burden bearers may receive wounds while healing
others and people suffer hurt when drained by spiritual leeches.

A leech is the opposite of a burden bearer. A leech is a person
who does not pay the price of prayer to sustain his own life and
perhaps fails to maintain emotional or mental hygiene and discipline as well. The leech therefore sustains himself by drawing on
the strength of others. This person too needs to find balance and
healing—letting go of fears and finding strength in the One who

can truly sustain him. "The leech has two daughters, 'Give,' 'Give,'" (Prov. 30:15). At times, all of us need to lean on our brothers and sisters. God has designed us to give and receive strength and comfort from one another.

> Blessed be the God and Father of our Lord Jesus Christ, the Father of mercies and God of all comfort; who comforts us in all our affliction so that we may be able to comfort those who are in any affliction with the comfort with which we ourselves are comforted by God. For just as the sufferings of Christ are ours in abundance, so also our comfort is abundant through Christ. But if we are afflicted, it is for your comfort and salvation; or if we are comforted, it is for your comfort, which is effective in the patient enduring of the same sufferings which we also suffer.
>
> —2 CORINTHIANS 1:3–6

It is good to give and receive comfort one to another. By such sharing, our love for one another in Christ grows into the fullness St. Paul spoke of in Ephesians 4:11–16.

But leeches do not give back. They only drain. While true sharing of one another's sufferings is a gift of God by faith among those who have faith, leeching is a dead sucking of life by those who have insufficient faith to stand on their own two feet. Leeching is of the flesh, not of the Holy Spirit; it is a taking that prevents giving. Leeches hear Galatians 6:2 to mean that the body of Christ should bear their burden, not that they should bear the burdens of others. Leeches fail to heed Galatians 6:5, that each man bear his own load. With leeches there is no stopping place. They continually suck the energy of others, like vampires in the night.

WHAT IS BURDEN BEARING?

Burden bearing is predicated upon the capacity of our spirits to identify with one another, to empathize, to share and shoulder emotional loads. In the same way that two physically can carry a log that one alone cannot lift, burden bearing takes one end of a load and so enables a brother to survive and function.

Because we have seen how many in the body of Christ attempt to bear each others' burdens yet become overweighted, not understanding the full nature of what our Lord has called us to do, we feel that it is important to pause here and express to you what burden bearing actually is. This is an essential part of letting go of past ways of doing things and coming into the fullness of our new birth in Christ. Let's look at an illustration for how burden bearing should operate.

Suppose Bill (fictitious name) has a great number of problems. His emotions are in turmoil. His inner struggles are robbing his conscious mind of the ability to think clearly or even sometimes to remember what he was about to say. His mind tumbles and fumbles, trying to see a way out. His spirit is overloaded, and he can no longer pray effectively for himself.

God sees Bill's predicament and loves him—whether or not he has received Jesus as Savior or the baptism of the Holy Spirit. God the Father just simply loves. So, in our Lord Jesus Christ, He moves upon some Christians and calls them into prayer for Bill. By His Holy Spirit and through the invitation of His praying people, our Lord Jesus enters Bill's heart and becomes one with him. Then He begins to draw some of Bill's turmoil to His cross, through those who are praying. That is the work of burden bearing, as in Galatians 6:2, "Bear one another's burdens, and thus fulfill the law of Christ." Note that burden bearing is a supreme act of love, to love one another as He loved us, which is fulfilling the law of Christ. We shall see that this means to lay down our lives for one another, as He laid down His life for us.

The Lord will not draw all of Bill's suffering to Himself in that moment of intercession. Galatians 6:5 says, "For each one shall bear his own load." The Lord removes enough of the weight of Bill's turmoil so that he can again think clearly, settle his emotions, and do his own praying.

Burden bearing is solely the work of our Lord Jesus Christ, as Isaiah 53:4–5 says: "Surely our griefs He Himself bore, and our sorrows He carried; yet we esteemed Him stricken, smitten of God, and afflicted. But He was pierced through for our transgressions, He was crushed for our iniquities; the chastening for our well-being fell upon Him."

Burden bearing is not, "O God, give me my brother's pain." That is the heresy of substitution, as though we would substitute ourselves in place of Christ, playing God, as it were. It is the work of our Lord, who graciously invites us to share His sufferings (Phil. 3:10).

Burden bearing is a part of intercessory prayer, in which we respond to our Lord's call. He then enters in and draws our brother's or sister's pain to His cross through us. We may feel some of the distress—fear, anger, hurt, despondency, animosity, confusion, whatever troubles beset the other, as they go through us to the cross.

Jesus said, "He who has ears to hear, let him hear" (Matt. 11:15). When people are too beset with problems to hear, it is God's loving design to restore them to capacity through the intercessory burden-bearing prayers of those whom He calls to pray. Burden-bearing prayer is thus the precursor to individual healing and to revival. Romans 10:17 says, "So faith comes from hearing, and hearing by the word of Christ." But people—individuals, cities, regions, nations, and so on—often are too troubled and cannot hear. Then it is that the Lord needs an army of burden-bearing intercessors whose obedience can open hearts and minds to hear. Burden bearing is one of the first works that we can do to minister God's redemptive word and His healing touch to the world. But it is to be performed properly. Here's how.

How We Bear Burdens

We accomplish burden bearing first by obeying Romans 12:1: "I urge you therefore, brethren, by the mercies of God, to present your bodies a living and holy sacrifice, acceptable to God, which is your spiritual service of worship." We give ourselves to God and say, "You can lay anyone's burden in my heart, anytime, anywhere, and I will respond in prayer." Notice that it is our bodies that are to be given to God. It is in our bodies that we will feel the weight of burden bearing.

Next, we remain like minutemen, constantly and consciously ready to respond. The Lord then calls His servants in whatever way they are prepared to hear. He does it with Paula and me by causing us to feel something we know is not our own—someone's fear, hurt, or anger. We respond by entering into prayer, asking the Lord who is in trouble. Sometimes He tells us, and we have been known to call across the country to inquire of someone what's the matter that we have been called to pray. Often our Lord doesn't say; He just calls us to pray about whoever is hurting, inviting Him to act. That was His first purpose—to be given invitation through our response to the burden, to act in His redeeming saving grace.

We bear the burden to the cross, releasing it there. When it won't lift, we know either He is calling us to travail awhile longer, or something in us needs to die so we can let go of the burden more easily. We pray accordingly.

It is an inexpressible joy and privilege to be a burden bearer for the Lord, as further testimony will reveal. For now, suffice it to say we believe burden bearing to be a most important—and little known and thus neglected—part of our ongoing life in Christ. Our fervent prayer is that you will understand and respond. The need for burden-bearing intercessors, especially at this moment in history, cannot be overstated.

THE STRENGTH OF CONNECTION THROUGH BURDEN BEARING

Whereas two must be in proximity to lift something physically, burden bearing requires no spatial nearness. We can feel, identify, share, and pray about another's burdens at whatever distance we may happen to be. When we are apart or for some other reason cannot communicate with brothers or sisters in Christ, we may shoulder their burdens but be unable to identify what the burden is or which person's burden we are carrying. That hurts, for we hunger for knowledge.

> But we, brethren, having been bereft of you for a short while—*in person, not in spirit*—were all the more eager with great desire to see your face. For we wanted to come to you—I, Paul, more than once—and yet Satan thwarted us. For who is our hope or joy or crown of exultation? Is it not even you, in the presence of our Lord Jesus at His coming? For you are our glory and joy. Therefore *when we could endure it no longer,* we

thought it best to be left behind at Athens alone; and we sent Timothy, our brother and God's fellow worker in the gospel of Christ, to strengthen and encourage you as to your faith.
—1 Thessalonians 2:17–3:2, emphasis added

Any burden bearer who has carried another in his heart knows by experience the weight of Paul's words, "when we could endure it no longer." We *can* endure mere curiosity about our brother's welfare, but love and concern for the other nearly overwhelms us when we are bearing burdens and can obtain no news. We hunger desperately to hear how that one is. Knowledge enables us to pray specifically and to release burdens to the Lord. Lacking that, we continue to labor.

Throughout the New Testament we are commanded to love one another. We all know that. But what does that really mean? What do we do that is uniquely, peculiarly love for our brother? James gave us part of the answer. "If a brother or sister is without clothing and in need of daily food, and one of you says to them, 'Go in peace, be warmed and be filled,' and yet you do not give them what is necessary for their body, what use is that?" (James 2:15–16). John echoed that in 1 John 3:16–18: "We know love by this, that He laid down His life for us; and we ought to lay down our lives for the brethren. But whoever has the world's goods, and beholds his brother in need and closes his heart against him, how does the love of God abide in Him? Little children, let us not love with word or with tongue, but in deed and truth." Love is therefore not so much a feeling in the heart as it is a matter of specific actions. We learn in other places that such actions are composed of forgiving, preferring others' interests before our own (Phil. 2:4), not insisting on our own way (1 Cor. 13:5), and that love "bears all things, believes all things, hopes all things, endures all things" (1 Cor. 13:7).

Love can be classified in two ways: nonaggressive and aggressive. Nonaggressive love can be shown by our self-discipline not to act in any way that could harm someone else, which I call forbearing love, and by our desire to spend ourselves in prayer to forgive others when they hurt us. Aggressive love, on the other hand, is composed of activities that cause us to take positive steps in actions to benefit others.

A CROSS TO BEAR

Intercessory burden bearing is intentional, aggressive action taken for others. It is, in fact, cross bearing. We commonly say, "Oh, that brother has a cross to bear," or "What a cross I have to carry!" But let us free our Christian mentality from false usages. Troubles and tragedies that befall us are not crosses to bear. They are simply and only that, troubles and sorrows that test and refine us. Nor is the abuse we take from relatives or friends "a cross to bear." Difficult people or circumstances are what the Bible calls our "thorns in the flesh" (Num. 33:55; 2 Cor. 12:7). They are not crosses to bear. *Nothing that involuntarily befalls us is a cross to bear.* Cross bearing involves at least three aspects peculiar to itself.

1. Cross bearing is volitional.

First, it is volitional. The cross did not happen *to* Jesus. He *accomplished* it. "And behold, two men were talking with Him; and they were Moses and Elijah, who, appearing in glory, were speaking of His departure which He was about to *accomplish* at Jerusalem" (Luke 9:30–31, emphasis added). "Jesus said to them

'My food is to do the will of Him who sent Me, and to accomplish His work'" (John 4:34). That work was to die on the cross, where He cried out that the work of redemption was accomplished: "It is finished!" (John 19:30). Being volitional, cross bearing is also purposeful. "Now My soul has become troubled; and what shall I say, 'Father, save Me from this hour'? But for this *purpose* I came to this hour" (John 12:27, emphasis added). The cross is love in action in which Christians purposefully, knowingly lay down their lives for others.

2. Cross bearing is redemptive suffering.

The second peculiar aspect of cross bearing is that it is redemptive suffering. Simple reaping of suffering because we deserve it is in no way to be identified as "a cross I have to bear." It is disgraceful to think of our well-merited suffering as a cross because we would not repent and let Jesus bear it on the cross for us. In this case, we suffer because of our sin, not for righteousness' sake.

Some may question whether, since Jesus has accomplished all on the cross, it is scriptural, or wise, to think of any human being other than Jesus as suffering redemptively for one another. But this is another of those areas in our Lord's wisdom in which only "both/and" rather than "either/or" thinking ought to be applied. He did accomplish all. Redemption is a finished work. We cannot add one iota to His perfected work of salvation. On the other hand, in His wisdom and in the mystery of time, He intends to continue that work of redemptive suffering through the body of Christ. We are here to magnify rather than augment, His saving work. How else can we comprehend St. Paul's statement: "Now I rejoice in my sufferings *for your sake*, and in my flesh I do share on behalf of His body (which is the church) in filling up *that which is lacking* in

Christ's afflictions" (Col. 1:24, emphasis added)? We find the same way of thinking in 2 Corinthians 4:10–12:

> [We are] *always carrying about in the body the dying of Jesus,* that the life of Jesus also may be manifested in our body. For we who live are constantly being delivered over to death for Jesus' sake, that the life of Jesus also may be manifested in our mortal flesh. *So death works in us, but life in you.*
>
> —EMPHASIS ADDED

As we will see more fully later, redemptive suffering for others is not only possible and scriptural, but it is also commanded by our Lord Himself. (See Galatians 6:2; John 15:13–16.)

Cross bearing is redemptive suffering for others, purposefully, willingly undertaken in obedience to our Lord Jesus Christ. It should be understood that redemptive suffering for others cannot be accomplished by our flesh, nor indeed by us at all. Redemption is the providence of Jesus, and Jesus only. It is Jesus who, *in us,* suffers redemptively for others. It is in Him that we bear burdens. If we are not in Him, we only worry in the flesh. We bear whatever burden He bears in us so long as He chooses to bear it in us—and not one second longer—else we need the healing of which we will write later in this chapter. St Paul said we share in the "fellowship of His sufferings, being conformed to His death" (Phil. 3:10). In His wisdom, our Lord allows us to share in miniscule portions His redemptive suffering for humanity.

To us, that is what is meant by the phrase so often quoted, "to minister to the Lord." We may minister to others in many ways, but it seems to us that only those who have learned to bear His burdens with Him truly minister to the Lord Himself. And what a blessing and a joy that is!

3. Cross bearing is like death.

The third aspect peculiar to cross bearing is death. Mere personal pain may or may not bring death of self, depending on our faith and comprehension. But that kind of death of self is only our own crucifixion, for our sin, for our own salvation's sake. *Cross bearing is unique in that death is entered for the sake of others.* Whatever personal death we may come to because of what trials come upon us, let us never seek to ennoble that as cross bearing. Although we die our own personal death *upon* the cross, we *bear* the cross for others. Our own death does not participate in such glory. How often St. Paul said that what he did or what he suffered was "for your sakes" (Col. 1:24; 2 Cor. 4:12, 15). St. Paul wanted his friends to know that what he suffered was not for himself but in love for them, or for Jesus' sake: "For we who live are constantly being delivered over to death *for Jesus'* sake" (2 Cor. 4:11, emphasis added). "For to you it has been granted *for Christ's sake*, not only to believe in Him, *but also to suffer for His sake*, experiencing the same conflict which you saw in me, and now hear to be *in* me" (Phil. 1:29–30, emphasis added).

Hear again 2 Corinthians 4:12: "So death works *in* us, but life *in* you." Note that it does not say death working *upon* us, but it says death working *in* us. In burden bearing, we take another's death *into* ourselves. More accurately, our Lord reaches from His cross through our hearts and spirits to draw our brother's death to Himself on the cross. Suffering that does not involve this altruistic sharing of another's death for His sake is neither intercessory burden bearing nor cross bearing.

At one time in my meditations, I was wrestling with these matters when the Lord said to me, "Look up Romans 8:1–4." So I did. This is one of those familiar passages we have all read so many times that we are sure we understand, and therefore we don't at all! The Lord proceeded to reveal this to me. I thought, "Oh, yes, Lord. That means that because I have accepted you as my Lord and Savior, I am free from sin and death."

He said, "Yes, Paul did say that, in many places, but that is not what he was saying here." So I looked again, and saw "Spirit" in verse 2.

"Oh yes, Lord, since I have the baptism of the Holy Spirit, I am free from sin and death." And now I had scriptural warrant. I quoted, "And where the Spirit of the Lord is, there is freedom" (2 Cor. 3:17, NIV).

"Yes, John," He responded. "The Holy Spirit does bring freedom, and St. Paul did say that, in many ways. But that is not what he was saying here. Look again."

So I looked again, and this time He caused passages to leap off the pages into my eyes. "For the *law of the Spirit of life* in Christ Jesus has set you free from the *law of sin* and of death" (Rom. 8:2, emphasis added). Oh! He wasn't speaking here only of His blood and His cross, nor of the Holy Spirit primarily, but also about the *law* of the Spirit of life and the *law* of sin and death!

"Well then, what is the law of sin and of death?" So He directed me to Romans 7, reminding me that when Paul wrote, there were no chapters or verse numbers; it all ran together as one message. Again, He caused the word *law* to leap off the page.

> For I joyfully concur with the *law* of God in the inner man, but I see a different *law* in the members of my body, waging war against the *law* of my mind, making me a prisoner of the *law* of sin which is in my members. Wretched man that I am! Who will set me free from the body of this death? Thanks be to God through Jesus Christ our Lord! So, then, on the one

hand I myself with my mind am serving the *law* of God, but on the other, with my flesh the *law* of sin.

—ROMANS 7:22–25

At last the Lord revealed to me what St. Paul was talking about. When we receive Jesus Christ as Lord and Savior, our sins are washed away and our flesh is dealt a deathblow. That begins the process of sanctification by which He daily brings us more and more to crucifixion in the practices of our flesh (Col. 3:9; Gal. 2:20; 5:24). Much of that death is accomplished by prayer for inner healing. But I had been agonizing over why so many receive much inner healing but never become whole. He was answering to say that there remains another crucial step that some take, and thereby become whole, and others do not. That is, to learn to live the "*law of the Spirit* of life in Christ Jesus." For yes, Christ has freed us *from* the prison of the law of sin, but He has also freed us *into* the law of the Spirit of life.

St. Paul, who was a scholar under Gamaliel, knew how to employ the word *law* in its strictly legal usages; here he was applying the word *law* in a most poetic, nonlegal way. That "different law in the members of my body, waging war against the *law* of my mind" the Lord revealed to me was another way of speaking of the flesh. The "body" St. Paul wanted to be set free from is not the physical body. He was using the word *body* in the same way we speak of a group of things as "the main body of the army" or a "body of people." "Who will set me free from this *body* of *death*" therefore means "Who will set me free from this body of many warring things in my flesh that continually re-entraps me in its old ways? How do I finally get free from the body of the world's ways in me to walk in the body of Christ's ways? How do I finally get free from the 'law' of the old way?" How? By learning and living a new "law," which replaces it!

First, we receive Jesus and are free from guilt. Then, we crucify the old man daily on the cross. We receive the law of the Spirit of life in Christ Jesus. But then we learn to live that law of love for others, which finally overcomes the old practices by building in the new *way* of Christ.

What, then, is "the law of the Spirit of life in Christ Jesus"? Jesus answered, "For whoever wishes to save his life shall lose it, but whoever loses his life for My sake, he is the one who will save it" (Luke 9:24). And in John 15:13, "Greater love has no one than this, that one *lay down his life* for his friends" (emphasis added). And in Luke 14:27, "Whoever does not carry *his own cross* and come after Me cannot be My disciple" (emphasis added). St. Paul said, "Bear one another's burdens, and thus fulfill *the law of Christ*" (Gal. 6:2, emphasis added). What is Christ's commandment? What is the law of Christ? "This is My commandment, that you love one another, just *as I have loved you*" (John 15:12, emphasis added). How did He love us? By laying down His life for us. St. Paul was saying in Romans 8 that we break free from our captivity to our old habits when we learn at last the law of Christ, to lay down our lives for others! It is not enough to take away sin and its practices. The new way of sacrificial love must be learned and lived.

But then the Lord told me, "You didn't understand what it is to lay down your life either, John!"

I thought, "Well, if I just lay down my selfish interests and my sins and spend some time helping others, that's laying down my life."

But the Lord said, "John, your selfishness and your sins are death, not life. I didn't say to lay down your death for others. I said to lay down your life."

So I thought, "If I lay down my time and energy for others and spend my life serving other people, surely that's what it is to lay down my life."

The Lord said, "No, your time and energy are not yet your life. I said to lay down your life."

"Well, what is my life?"

He said, "John, what was My life?" And then He opened the Scriptures to me as He had done for Cleopas and the other disciple on the road to Emmaus (Luke 24:27).

> I and the Father are one.
>
> —JOHN 10:30

> He who has seen Me has seen the Father.... The words that I say to you I do not speak on My own initiative, but the Father abiding in Me does His works.
>
> —JOHN 14:9–10

> And He who sent Me is with Me; He has not left Me alone, for I always do the things that are pleasing to Him.
>
> —JOHN 8:29

The life of Jesus was His relationship to His Father. He had left heaven to come to the earth, but He had never yet left His Father. "Wist ye not that I must be about my Father's business?" (Luke 2:49, KJV). When He was tired, He went to the mountains to be with His Father. That relationship with His Father, which was life itself to Him, was the very thing He was called upon to lay down!

> And if a man has committed a sin worthy of death, and he is put to death, and you hang him on a tree, his corpse shall not

hang all night on the tree, but you shall surely bury him the same day (*for he who is hanged is accursed of God*).
—DEUTERONOMY 21:22–23, EMPHASIS ADDED

In planning His own death on the cross, Jesus knew that the price to Him was to be far more than physical pain, which could only last a few hours at most. The inestimable cost to Him was to become our sin: "He made Him who knew no sin to be sin on our behalf, that we might become the righteousness of God in Him" (2 Cor. 5:21). Note carefully that Jesus was to become *sin, not sinful*. His own heart toward God remained pure. He remained the sinless, pure sacrificial Lamb of the Passover while filled with the sin of the world.

It should be said again that the word was *not* that He was to become *sinful*. He became able to bear our chastisement (Isa. 53:5) because He had become as us—He had become our *sin*. That is, He bore our sin much as a washcloth has taken into itself the filth it wipes up. However, He did not sin. "For we do not have a high priest who is unable to sympathize with our weaknesses, but we have one who has been tempted in every way, just as we are— *yet was without sin*" (Heb. 4:15, NIV, emphasis added).

A recent heresy took this teaching out of balance to the point of saying that He Himself needed redemption. A thousand times no! He was the spotless Lamb. In Himself He remained pure. It was our sin He carried to the cross. But He had to become like us in being "tempted in that which He has suffered" (Heb. 2:18). "My God, My God, why hast Thou forsaken Me?" (Matt. 27:46).

It could have meant little to Jesus to die physically. St. Paul said, "To die is gain" (Phil. 1:21). For Jesus, apart from our sin, to die would have been only to return His spirit to Him who gave it (Eccles. 12:7). Anticipating resurrection, that would have been joyful beyond measure to our Lord, the Son of God. The greater death, even for a short span, was to be filled all at once with the putrefaction of the wickedness of literally billions of souls! That was a far more important way to lay down His life, and the greatest cost to Jesus. It was for this reason far more than fear of physical suffering and death that He cried out for the cup, if possible, to be taken from Him (Matt. 26:39). Even that loss, the greatest death for Him, Jesus suffered for us.

What then is our life? What is it we are called to lay down for others? When we receive Jesus and are filled with the Holy Spirit, for the first time we have full access to the Father. We feel clean and good. "Who may ascend into the hill of the Lord? And who may stand in His holy place? He who has clean hands and a pure heart" (Ps. 24:3–4). Our hearts have been sprinkled with the blood of Jesus (Heb. 10:22). We delight to come into His presence in corporate worship and private devotions. Our hearts are freer and more open to share with brothers and sisters. That communion in Him and fellowship with our brothers and sisters have become our life, our joy. "For who is our hope or joy or crown of exultation? Is it not even you, in the presence of our Lord Jesus at His coming? For you are our glory and joy" (1 Thess. 2:19–20).

During the week we may become overburdened and borne down, but worship lifts us. His Word cleanses, and we are again free to reach out and touch the Lord and others. That is our life. The high we feel through that cleanliness, that capacity to hold the heart clean and open for the Lord and others, the wonderful feeling that flows from that life-giving ability to relate vulnerably and refreshingly with Him and others is the very thing He calls us to lay down in death for others!

We may leave an anointed service feeling refreshed and clean, like a radio freshly cleared of static to receive our wonderful Lord's broadcasts, only to run into a brother or sister at coffee hour who just has to tell us the latest juicy bit of gossip! In that moment we have a decision to make. The temptation is to hug our newly regained righteousness to ourselves, saying, "'God, I thank Thee that I am not like other people: swindlers, unjust, adulterers, or even like this tax-gatherer [how about inserting *slanderer* right there?]. I fast twice a week; I pay tithes of all that I get' (Luke 18:11–12). You've just washed me clean, Lord. I want to keep basking in that wonderful feeling." So we turn off. We reject that person. We give him or her the cold shoulder. That way we have not been like the Galilean Sea that receives refreshment from the mountains and pours it out to all the valley below. We have become like the Dead Sea that takes in all the Jordan can give and gives nothing out. We stagnate. We have not learned the lesson that he who would keep his life will lose it and he who would lose it will keep it.

The better decision would have been, "Lord, this child is hurting, or he wouldn't need to hurt others. I will open my heart and spirit to become one with him. I will let You, Lord, go through Gethsemane in me to absorb his hurt to Yourself and so set him free." In Gethsemane, Jesus entered into prayer, and as the God-man (not half-God, half-man, but fully God and fully man), He reached across time and space to become our rottenness, our doubt, our fear, our jealousy, our hate. He became everything that is sin in every person who then lived, had lived before, or would ever come to live on earth. That work was so exhausting that it broke His capillaries and He sweat blood (Luke 22:44), which means medically that He nearly died! The Father sent an angel to strengthen Him (v. 43). Peter, James, and John were so overcome by the burden of it they could not stay awake (Matt. 26:40–45).

Consider this: When Jesus left heaven to come to the earth, He became *a* man. But He yet remained *one* individual, by Himself. In the Garden of Gethsemane He became *mankind*. Until the agony He endured in the garden, His death on the cross might possibly have meant little, for He would only have died alone, as Himself only, affecting little other than by example. But when He became *as us*, then He was for the first time in position to reap on the cross as us for us. He had to become our sin in order to take on Himself all that we were due to reap.

Forgiveness is not God overlooking sin. Jesus came to fulfill the law, not to abolish it (Matt. 5:17). On the cross, because He had become as us in the garden of prayer, He fulfilled all the demands of the law for reaping. He could not have reaped our sin apart from us. The law does not work that way. He had to be *as us* to reap *for us*. Gethsemane was not a lapse into fear that Jesus overcame by prayer long enough to endure. Gethsemane was integrally necessary to the accomplishment of redemption by His death on the cross! Gethsemane was that requisite action of our Lord that purchased for Him the ability to pay the price for us. He had to become no longer one solitary saint but *as all* of us *for all* of us, or the cross could have had little more effect than that of the thousands who had already suffered similar deaths. Though He was God Himself, only *as us* could He ransom us. Only *as all of us* could He bear *all of our chastisement*. In Gethsemane He accomplished the work of empathetic identification, the work of burden bearing that made the cross effective.

We do not belabor this point for theological correction only. It is essential that those called to burden bearing comprehend His work in Gethsemane, for that is their primary calling and work. We are to prepare the way of the Lord (Isa. 40:3; Matt. 3:3).

How? What is it to prepare the way of the Lord? Many things, of course, like preaching, teaching, repenting, and so on. But the primary, prerequisite *preparation* is in the heart, by burden bearing. Hear the word *preparation*. Eventually, every person must make his own confession. But when their hearts are not free to do that, then only as Jesus reaches through willing hearts who will let Jesus identify with the sin of a brother or sister *in them can He effectively take enough of their imprisonment in their sin to His cross to set them sufficiently free to make their own confessions.*

When we do that, when we invite the Lord to draw another's death through our own body to His cross, that is what it is for a man to "carry his own cross" and so become Jesus's disciple (Luke 14:27).

When we offer ourselves to burden bearing, we may not feel as good as before. We hurt with our brother's hurt. We tremble with our sister's fear. We wrestle with our friend's anger. We struggle as if to overcome the jealousy that our neighbor suffers. We agonize with his doubts. We may temporarily lose our glibness before the Lord. We stammer and stutter and are weighed down with our friend's feelings of guilt and unworthiness. Our brother's death is truly in us in fact and in effect upon our heart and mind.

But that increases faith. We learn by practice to believe God is there, still blessing us fully, as His sweet presence suffuses the pain, bringing with it a richer communion with God than the "high" we previously felt. By losing our lives again and again, day in and day out, and regaining them just as often, we shatter dependence on highs. We know by more than belief. We *know* our lives in Him.

Burden bearers become obedient to the command of Romans 12:1: "I urge you therefore, brethren, by the mercies of God, to present your *bodies* a living and holy sacrifice, acceptable to God, which is your spiritual service of worship." Moreover, they come to understand it from within. The command was not to present the mind or heart or spirit as a living sacrifice, but the body, because it is our bodies that contain our minds, hearts, and spirits, and it is in the body that one bears "the burden and the scorching heat of the day" (Matt. 20:12).

Burden bearers realize by continual experience what those blessed words mean: *your spiritual service of worship.* Note how worship is connected to service. Often, the Church, like a spoiled child, wants only to sit on Daddy's lap and call that pleasing to Daddy's heart. But the Father would have been far better pleased by those children who hoed His garden and swept His house and then came for refreshment on His lap. The labor of burden bearing is itself our spiritual *service* of *worship.*

Paula and I said the same prayer every night for three years, not so much so that God who heard it for the first time would heed but so that every cell of our bodies would hear and receive: "Lord, we give You our heart, mind, body, soul, and spirit; our past; our present; our future; our ambition; and our destiny. We are Yours. Use us in any way You desire. You may lay any burden on us any time of the day or night, forever." Like bondservants, our ears are pierced through; we are His (Exod. 21:5–6).

Therefore the Lord has permission, and avails Himself of it, to involve us in sharing His burdens at any time, night or day. Paula may say to me, "Have you been feeling weighted down and fearful the last hour or so?" I say, "Yes, I have," and we enter prayer together to discover whose burden we are carrying or what to pray about. Or I may say, "Have you found yourself feeling angrier and angrier, and there's nothing to be angry about?" When she concurs (we almost always feel the same burdens at the same time), we proceed to prayer. Sometimes the burden of grief is so heavy in our chests we can hardly breathe. It is our Lord's grieving for the body. He stands in front of the tomb of some other Lazarus, who is more than four days dead in some stinking way, and weeps before He calls to life (John 11). But we are given the joy of participating with Him in His redemptive work, and there is also an undergirding sense of His peace and well-being that lies beneath the burden we carry for another.

What exactly does bearing our brother's death in us accomplish? It is one door, from heart to heart, by which Jesus can enter and heal. Since we live on Earth, and we are one with our brother, our prayer gives our courteous Lord permission and access to act.

One could ask, "Why did Jesus come to Earth at all? Why didn't He just wipe out sin and Satan from heaven?" The answer is, among other things, free will. He had to come and be one of us in order to gain access and permission. My brother's free will still means that our Lord's access to his life is limited, though the Lord possesses all the power of the universe. The Lord has returned to heaven; His body remains here. The degree then that my heart, as a fellow human being, becomes as my brother's heart is the degree to which our Lord can begin to deliver him from whatever his problem is.

The Holy Spirit knows the stopping places. He knows Galatians 6:5 ("for each one shall bear his own load") as well as He knows Galatians 6:2 ("bear one another's burdens"), and He stops the burden bearing at that point when our brother must make his own invitation and bear his own load. But my heart prepares the way of the Lord to my brother's heart. I carry that which would crush and defeat without redemptive effect. I lighten my brother's load until he can stand free in Jesus.

There is no poesy involved in "and if one member suffers, all the members suffer with it; if one member is honored, all the members rejoice with it" (1 Cor. 12:26). St. Paul was describing the fact of our mutual existence. We *are* that corporate. We all rejoice and grieve unceasingly as we live among our neighbors. "For by what he saw and heard that righteous man, *while living among them, felt his righteous soul tormented day after day* with their lawless deeds" (2 Pet. 2:8, emphasis added). Burden bearers are not merely subject by virtue of existence to the hurts of others. When the Lord prompts, they consciously invite more than they would have received incidentally by "living among them." They seek out the hurt in order to transmit it to the Lord.

Burden bearers receive several rewards distinctive to their labor. We all want to be where Jesus is. Our hymns celebrate an eternity of being with Him. But until eternity, how shall we abide in Him and so bear much fruit (John 15:4)? We must go where Jesus goes. Jesus is the water of life. Water flows downhill. If we would be where Jesus is, then we must seek Him where He is always going—to the lowest point of suffering, hurt, fear, death, and shame! By suffering *with* Him for others, burden bearers learn what it is to truly abide in Him. Jesus ceases to be their Santa Claus, a means merely to procure good gifts for their own selfish lives. He becomes their life, poured out for others. Burden bearers are privileged to experience the reality of Jesus in a far deeper way, because Christ is invited to continue His work of redemption in and through them. They know no separation from Him because He always lives to work the Father's good pleasure in them (Phil. 2:13). They do not measure His presence or proximity by ephemeral feelings. They *know* whom they have believed because they work with Him every day.

Burden bearers progress more quickly in their own sanctification by crucifixion. If the Lord has dealt with an area of my heart, and if I identify with the hurt and sin of a brother in some similar or identical area, I am transparent. The yoke is easy and the burden is light, as it ought to be (Matt. 11:30). It passes through me to the cross without interference. But if I identify with some sinful characteristic in a brother and my own heart yet retains the same or similar undealt-with sin in my flesh, then "gunk" gets stuck in me! My brother's hurt and sin do not pass easily and lightly through me to the cross. His sin now sits heavily upon my heart, and I am forced to see my own sin. That, happening so often as it does, drives me to my own death on the cross. I cannot fool myself and congratulate myself that I have dealt with sin in an area that my brother's sin lingers and will not depart to the cross. Thus the labor of laying down my life to bear death for others also brings me to my own confession and death.

Burden bearers come to know Jesus better than all the others who have not yet responded to that call. The more we bear the burden of others, the more we feel the weight and horror of sin. Therefore the more we begin to sense the price our Lord pays for our very continued existence! We see in real terms the love of Jesus each moment of time in action to save. We see how if Jesus stopped interceding before the Father, the weight of mankind's sin would destroy the earth in thirty seconds! Our heart becomes enraptured in love and awe for Him. Until we begin, in whatever tiniest modicum He allows, to experience His suffering for others, we have no way to truly appreciate His continual gift of redemptive suffering for all mankind every moment of life!

Listen to how beautifully St. Paul said it:

More than that, I count all things to be loss in view of *the surpassing value of knowing Christ Jesus my Lord,* for whom I have suffered the loss of all things, and count them but rubbish in order that I may gain Christ, and may be found in Him, not having a righteousness of my own derived from the Law, but that which is through faith in Christ, the righteousness which comes from God on the basis of faith, *that I may know Him,* and the power of His resurrection *and the fellowship of His sufferings, being conformed to His death;* in order that I may attain to the resurrection from the dead.

—PHILIPPIANS 3:8–11, EMPHASIS ADDED

If anyone already knew Jesus, St. Paul did. But there is more to know. St. Paul was the very one who preached most about the *free gift* of eternal life, but here he said, "I may *attain* to the resurrection from the dead." We submit that in this instance St. Paul was not speaking at all about going to heaven. We have nothing to do to "attain" heaven other than to receive Jesus. He is our simple ticket home to eternity. We need do nothing else. St. Paul was speaking about attaining to the fullness of resurrection life here and now! He went on to say he was forgetting everything else in order to "press on toward the goal for the prize of the upward call of God in Christ Jesus" (v. 14). Many Christians have striven with utmost zeal for the same goal, only never to escape self-centered striving for personal perfection, a striving that can end only in Phariseeism and misery! Burden bearers learn the secret of life, which is to lose life in order to find it. They swim in the fullness of the stream that refreshes the city of God (Ps. 46:4). Others try to find their own life and lose it. Burden bearers forget about themselves by becoming so focused on helping carry others' burdens to the cross that the life of Jesus fills and refreshes faster than they can pour it out. Their cruse of oil, poured out in the Elijah task, can never be emptied, for they walk in the lifestyle of Jesus. They begin to enter into the sweetness of resurrection life here and now.

Burden bearers come eventually to an even sweeter reward. They come to know the Father God as Jesus knows Him, and Father God abides in their heart. (I repeat here a testimony given in *The Elijah Task*, chapter 9, and in several tapes, for the reason that it is the *summum bonum* of a burden bearer's life. As such, it is not only appropriate but also the climax of any text on burden bearing.)

One night I (John) was driving home from Spokane. I was alone on the freeway when there came a tap on my shoulder—a very real physical tap. Nearly audibly the Lord said, "John?"

I said, "Yes, Lord."

He said, "I have someone I want you to meet."

I said, "Yes, Lord."

"I want you to meet My Father."

"Yes, Lord."

The next second, pouring over me was the most wonderful, gracious, tender, safe, and secure presence I had ever experienced. As one can know a multitude of things in a split second, I knew that this was not a passing experience. Although Father God had entered my heart on the day I became a Christian, my heart now knew more deeply than ever that Father God had come to stay. In that same instant I knew Father God was not at all like my childish reading of the Old Testament had said He was when I read how God was angry when Saul failed to kill all those Amalekites (1 Sam. 15). Father God was perfect, tender loving-kindness. I knew in that moment that the battle and the search were over. From that moment on, Father God *had* me, and nothing could be more wonderful. I felt safe, at rest, and secure. I could do nothing but hang onto the wheel, grateful that in His wisdom He had come when the freeway was empty, and cry out, over and over, "Oh, Father." I *knew* why St. Paul had written, "You have received a spirit of adoption as sons by which we cry out, 'Abba! Father!'" (Rom. 8:15). For two weeks I staggered around overwhelmed by the Father's loving presence and knew firsthand what the Scripture means when it says, "God *is love*" (1 John 4:8, emphasis added), "God is light, and in Him *there is no darkness at all*" (1 John 1:5, emphasis added), and "Every good thing bestowed and every perfect gift is from above, coming down from the *Father* of lights, with whom *there is no variation, or shifting shadow*" (James 1:17, emphasis added).

By then, however, I had been down so many seemingly good blind alleys and suffered so many misleading mystical experiences, that though I was certain this was what it seemed to be, I wasn't going to have even this wonderful gift unless the Lord could show it to me in Scripture, and I said so. He replied, "John, look up John 14:21." Knowing I was driving and that it was nighttime, He simply quoted it for me. (Isn't it great that the Lord knows Scripture!) "He who has My commandments and keeps them, he it is who loves Me; and he who loves Me shall be loved by My Father, and I will love him, and will disclose Myself to him"—the very things we have been teaching, that His commandments are to lay down our lives for our friends, to love as He has loved! Here He was adding that such burden bearing is the very prerequisite to arrival in a special relationship with the Father. Jesus was saying that one really does come to know Him and He is disclosed when one shares His suffering for others, keeping the commandment of Galatians 6:2!

Stubbornly I said, "That's not enough, Lord."

He said, "Look up John 14:23." Again He quoted it, "If anyone loves Me, he will keep My word; and My Father will love him, and *We* will come to him, and *make Our abode* with him" (emphasis added). This was the very thing that was just happening to me! My heart swelled, and my mind fairly burst with light. My thoughts were saying, "Oh, yes, I see. I see. Why did I never see it before?" But to the Lord I said, more humbly but as determinedly, "That's still not enough, Lord." So He quoted to me all of Ephesians 3:14–19.

> For this reason, I bow my knees before the Father, from whom every family in heaven and on earth derives its name, that He would grant you, according to the riches of His glory, to be strengthened with power through His Spirit in the inner man; so that Christ may dwell in your hearts through faith; and that you, being rooted and grounded in love, *may be able to comprehend* with all the saints what is the breadth and length and height and depth, and *to know the love of Christ* which surpasses knowledge, *that you may be filled up to all the fullness of God.*
>
> —EMPHASIS ADDED

Then, while I basked in the Father's presence and drove slowly on, Jesus taught me. He said, "John, when you received Me as Lord and Savior, I entered with My Father and with the Holy Spirit. Implicitly, you possessed all three of Us then. You soon learned you needed to experience the Holy Spirit explicitly. But I came with the Holy Spirit precisely in order to restore you to My Father! That's My purpose. You needed to experience the Father explicitly, too. Burden bearing is the way you or anyone comes into 'the fullness of God.'"

I remembered then that "no one can come to Me, unless the Father who sent Me draws him" (John 6:44), and more to the point, "no one comes to the Father, but through Me" (John 14:6). Jesus the Son had just drawn me to the Father. In the process He had taught me that burden bearing is not merely the work of a few adepts who happen to have a strange and different gift. It is the province and calling of every Christian—the very prerequisite to coming into fullness of life with God the Father for every Christian!

Since that time I have been far more at peace and rest. I *know* Father God has me. The search is over. I know if I fall, Father God will pick me up. I know the source of power. Jesus said, "The words that I say to you I do not speak on My own initiative, but the Father abiding in Me does His works" (John 14:10). It is the Father who sent Jesus who sends us all. It is the Father who works in Him who works in me. I do not have to strive to make anything happen. It is the Father's work and His responsibility. I only have the joy of serving the most compassionate, tender, safe, and loving Father who ever was.

Burden bearing is the key to fullness of life. We cannot arrive merely by coming into the Father's house and celebrating how good it is to be saved. Worship without service eventually hears again the prophet's cry:

> When you come to appear before Me,
> Who requires of you this trampling of My courts?
> Bring your worthless offerings no longer,
> Incense is an abomination to Me.
> New moon and sabbath, the calling of assemblies—
> I cannot endure iniquity and the solemn assembly.
> I hate your new moon festivals and your appointed feasts,
> They have become a burden to Me.
> I am weary of bearing them.
> So when you spread out your hands in prayer,

I will hide My eyes from you,
Yes, even though you multiply prayers, I will not listen.
Your hands are covered with blood.
Wash yourselves, make yourselves clean;
Remove the evil of your deeds from My sight.
Cease to do evil,
Learn to do good; seek justice,
Reprove the ruthless;
Defend the orphan,
Plead for the widow.

—ISAIAH 1:12–17

Paula and I can confidently say, after serving as prayer ministers for more than forty years, that the central sin behind all sin-caused suffering in human life is one simple thing—self-centered selfishness! By that we do not mean stinginess. Generous, ever-giving people may yet remain self-centered, so long as those services originate in their definition of themselves as loving people rather than in the Holy Spirit's outpouring of Jesus's life. Among those who remain self-centered, their good deeds arise from their need to fulfill their picture of themselves rather than from the Lord's calling. Such good deeds often bother people more than they help.

Self-centered selfishness continues at the center of our being long after our sins are washed away, long after the flesh receives its initial deathblow, and even long after we begin to learn to lay down our life in burden bearing! Salvation is a process, positionally begun and ended at conversion, but it is worked out in fear and trembling:

So then, my beloved, just as you have always obeyed, not as in my presence only, but now much more in my absence, *work out your salvation with fear and trembling.*

—PHILIPPIANS 2:12, EMPHASIS ADDED

In this you greatly rejoice, even though now for a little while, if necessary, you have been distressed by various trials, that the proof of your faith, being more precious than gold which is perishable, even though tested by fire, may be found to result in praise and glory and honor at the revelation of Jesus Christ; and though you have not seen Him, you love Him, and though you do not see Him now, but believe in Him, you greatly rejoice with joy inexpressible and full of glory, *obtaining as the outcome of your faith the salvation of your souls.*

—1 PETER 1:6–9, EMPHASIS ADDED

We must persevere in burden bearing until it becomes more than an occasional thing we just happen to remember to do. Burden bearing must become an automatic, unconscious built-in lifestyle. Only so does the work of it become enough and so engrossing as to overcome the core of our self-centeredness and so set us free. St. Paul wrote, "We have come to share in Christ *if* we hold firmly till the end the confidence we had at first" (Heb. 3:14, NIV, emphasis added). The body has come to understand that to mean that we must grit our teeth and hang onto our belief until the end. St. Paul meant much more. He wrote that in the context of Hebrews 4, which is the chapter about entering into *His rest,* "There remains therefore a Sabbath rest for the people of God. For the one who has entered His rest has himself also rested from his works, as God did from His" (Heb. 4:9–10). The principal work that our self-centered hearts must lay down and cease doing is our perpetual striving to build, defend, and live for our own self-image. *Whoever holds his confidence in himself long enough to persevere in fleshly burden bearing until fatigue crushes him discovers he can no longer bear burdens as a part of fulfilling his own self-image.* Love for and desire to bear burdens must come to death by the continual weight of it, until one does it only by obedience, letting the Lord do it in us, as us, for us. That death brings us both freedom and rest. Romans 7 and 8 and Hebrews 3 and 4 become one message, written on our hearts, when burden bearing, by obedience alone, finally slays self-centeredness at its core. We enter the freedom of Romans 8. We abide in the restfulness of Hebrews 4.

Even so, all I need to do is to become tired of burden bearing, refuse a few callings of the Lord, and my selfishness reasserts itself. I must either walk in Jesus's continual self-giving, or my self-taking reassumes command of me and I fall from rest to self-centered striving all over again. Burden bearing, laying down life for others, is thus not a nice option. It is the quintessential sacrificial life that alone ensures death and thus life, for every Christian.

Oh, that the body of Christ would hear the call of the Lord to service and take up the service of burden bearing. We cannot continually celebrate that we are going to heaven while the fields are white unto harvest and salvation is only begun, not ended. Let's learn that which truly brings us into the fullness. Burden bearing is not, as we have thought, the province of those few unfortunate weirdos who happen to be sensitive to what others feel. Although this chapter focuses on those whose naturally sensitive temperaments predispose them toward use of the supernatural gifts of the Spirit, one does not have to be able to sense pain across space in order to bear burdens. Ordinary everyday empathy will suffice, whether expressed through a hand on the shoulder or a listening ear. It is the *first calling* and *primary labor* of *every* Christian, the very *life/breath* of the *normal Christian life*, the way by which we come into the fullness of relationship with the Father and into sufficient death of self to enter freedom and rest. It is simple—respond and serve, or fail to enter the fullness.

PITFALLS IN BURDEN BEARING

Having said all those good things about burden bearing, we must now look at the other side, for there are pitfalls. Burden bearing is not always safe, either from what may be encountered or from one's own flesh. Temptations are always present—temptations to do too much, to take oneself too seriously, to judge and blame, to become overburdened and confused, to think of one's own problems as someone else's, or vice versa.

Often, in prayer ministry, Paula and I discover natural burden bearers who have never understood what their spirits have leaped into, uninformed and unaided. These people enter a room and almost instantly sense and take on nearly everyone's burden. Their hearts reach out instinctively to enfold and comfort. For many such people, life becomes too heavy a burden.

I speak from painful experience. I cannot remember when I was not like that. When the fullness of the Holy Spirit came, the burden of it became too much. I couldn't control it, much less stop it. In worship services and prayer meetings, others would be rejoicing, smiling, and laughing, while I sank in sorrow as I sopped up the hurts they were not letting themselves feel. I would try to be happy, but my smile would freeze and fade. I could not be happy. Eventually, the Lord gloriously healed that, as we will share presently.

Natural burden bearers become wounded spirits unless fortunate enough to find instruction and the protection of wiser friends. Their lack of understanding throws them into hurtful strivings of the flesh. What should be easy, light, and joyous (as Jesus said in Matthew 11:30) becomes heavy and oppressive. If they happen also to be performance-oriented people, as I was, they try too hard and take to heart each failure to help others and so become loaded with false guilt. If they happen to be parentally inverted like me, they can't let go and rest. The whole world seems to rest on their shoulders.

Burden bearers often pick up on sorrow and hurt in their friends when their friends are laughing and totally convinced that they are happy.

A wise proverb says, "Knowledge increases sorrow." Burden bearers live with the loneliness of knowing things others do not know and may not want or be able to bear. If a burden bearer lacks ego strength (courage of spirit), he may become confused and uncertain about his own perceptions. If he is arrogant and insensitive to how others may receive what he says, he may confuse, anger, or wound others by blurting out his perceptions without wisdom.

People may become afraid of such a person. So often I asked people why they felt the way they did when they thought they had their feelings well hidden, and so frequently I added a bit of perception or the gift of knowledge that many in our town became afraid of me! "He knows too much." "He's got X-ray eyes." "I feel like he's looking right through me." That wounds the spirit of both the friends and the burden bearer. On the other hand, if sensitivity to the fears of others caused me not to ask questions, that stuck me with too many heavy and unidentifiable burdens. I felt like Jeremiah: "But if I say, 'I will not remember Him or speak anymore in His name,' then in my heart it becomes like a burning fire shut up in my bones; and I am weary of holding it in, and I cannot endure it" (Jer. 20:9).

Most often we have found such natural burden bearers driven into silence and loneliness. They have learned in pain not to share. Others didn't understand, or they denied their perceptions, or they were affronted as though they had been some kind of spiritual voyeurs, peeping behind curtains that ought to have remained drawn. Of course, sometimes this accusation was hurtfully true, for the Holy Spirit is a perfect gentleman; He respects privacy, but our flesh does not.

Some burden bearers are immature, acting in the flesh, or even unconverted. Some become enamored of their gift or love the feeling of power and so unwittingly enlist the aid of demons. In the end, their gift turns from burden bearing to suspicion and gossip. In short, burden bearing without instruction and propriety in the Holy Spirit wounds the personal spirits both of the burden bearer and his "victim." Both need healing, which is done by simple investigative inquiry and prayer asking Jesus to heal and restore.

I leaped characteristically whole hog into burden bearing, long before I had gained any tact or wisdom in the Holy Spirit or had learned about proper separation of the functions of soul and spirit. It became utterly oppressive. I experienced flesh fatigue that produced only pride in my own false martyrdom. The Holy Spirit in me would only have taken on those burdens in people that Jesus was at that moment enduring. But the flesh leaped grandly to do everything all at once and congratulated itself that the fatigue was for Him and the adverse reactions of some people were noble persecutions to be reveled in. In time, however, the game became too crushing, and I had to look honestly at myself. The Lord sent Winston Nunes, a brother who explained separation of the functions of soul and spirit to me and prayed me through.

Soul and spirit cannot be separated in terms of space but in terms of function. "For the word of God is living and active and sharper than any two-edged sword, and piercing as far as the division of soul and spirit, of both joints and marrow, and able to judge the thoughts and intentions of the heart" (Heb. 4:12). Brother Winston explained that the Lord has built us like an automobile engine, which has separate places for oil, water, and gasoline. If water enters where gasoline or oil should be, gasoline where oil or water should be, or oil where water or gasoline operates, trouble ensues. Just so, God designed the mind to do certain tasks, the heart others, and the spirit others still. But the Fall so scrambled us that emotions flood beyond their bounds and adversely affect or sometimes fully overcome the mind and spirit. Similarly the mind can stifle emotions or block the spirit, and the spirit can run amok beyond the controls of the mind, causing us to sail into far-out experiences. He explained that after conversion, we need prayer to unscramble our inner beings and settle the functions of our parts, each into its own sphere. If soul and spirit are properly settled into separate functions, then our Lord can lay a burden into our spirit and we are not torn up everywhere all at once. Our own emotions and thoughts remain undisturbed, though participating. We maintain sufficient detachment to identify, pray, and remain in balance. If our hearts and minds become engaged in a problem, our spirits remain at peace. Each part properly supplies its contribution without overriding the functions of other parts. We enter another dimension of the rest spoken of in Hebrews 4 because our emotions no longer run amok, our minds no longer overcontrol, and our spirits do not splay themselves out, unguarded by the mind and heart.

When Winston Nunes prayed over me that the Lord separate the functions of my soul and spirit and bring to death the overstirrings of my flesh, it was as though he had lifted a thousand-pound weight from my shoulders! I came home light and free as a bird! No longer did I have to bear burdens Jesus did not require of me. No more did my own emotions and mentality become garbled. Each part of me could work in cooperation with each other part. Even my health and physical coordination as an athlete dramatically improved.

There are countless natural burden bearers staggering around without an informed Christian to teach them and set them free. Paula and I have discovered hundreds and have had the joy in the Lord of setting them free as our Lord did through Winston for me.

Then our delightfully humorous Lord set about through His own ways to "restore to me the joy of Thy salvation" (Ps. 51:12). Pat Brooks wrote a book entitled *Out in Jesus' Name*. I took exception to some things in her book, and for the first time in my life I wrote a critique and sent it to her.

I wrote in longhand, and, not having her address, sent it to her publisher to be forwarded. Not being able to decipher my chicken scratchings, the publisher thought it was addressed to Pat Boone and sent it on to him! Pat found himself bemused, unable to apply the contents to his book, but he was intrigued by the comments. He took the letter to his pastor, Jack Hayford, and the two of them discerned that I lacked the gift of joy! Whereupon they prayed for me to have that gift!

One morning subsequently, the Lord held His usual discussion with me: "You didn't understand that Scripture." This time it was to say that I missed the point of the verse we sing, "The joy of the Lord is my strength" (from Nehemiah 8:10). Nearly audibly He said, "John, you thought that meant you had to have some joy in order to be strong. So you tried to stir some up. And every time you failed to feel joy because you were overburdened with My sorrows, you felt you had failed and put yourself under condemnation. But you didn't really see what it said." He went on to tell me, "It says, 'the joy of the Lord.' It is My joy that is your strength, not yours. You tried to be joyful and couldn't. But you didn't understand. Where do I live, John?"

"In me," I answered.

"John, I always have joy, whether you do or not. Therefore, My joy is always in you, whether you feel it or not. It is My joy that is your strength!"

The next morning Paula and I had one of those rare moments for us when everything we said and did went at cross-purposes. I had just told the Lord I wasn't too happy with His gift to me and I wasn't too happy with Him either, when the first carload of people coming for ministry appeared in the driveway. I walked out to greet them, still murmuring under my breath. The first one stepped out of the car and exclaimed, "Oh, John, the joy of the Lord is just pouring out of you this morning!"

I thought, "That's just the trouble. It's pouring out!" But the Lord said, "Do you see, John? My joy is always there, and when you least feel it, others can still see it pouring out!" At last I believed and came to rest. I didn't have to experience it all the time to believe that His joy was still my joy and my strength.

The Lord then opened Ecclesiastes 7:2–4 to me.

> It is better to go to a house of mourning
> Than to go to a house of feasting,
> Because that is the end of every man,
> And the living takes it to heart.
> Sorrow is better than laughter,
> For when a face is sad a heart may be happy.

The mind of the wise is in the house of mourning,
While the mind of fools is in the house of pleasure.

The Lord applied that to entering into the chore of burden bearing as contrasted to remaining in the house of self-centered celebrating. He explained it to me like Walt Whitman: "Do I contradict myself? / Very well then I contradict myself, / (I am large, I contain multitudes.)"[1] Since my soul and spirit contain separate functions, I could enter sorrow in burden bearing and rejoice with Him in the labor of it on a deeper level in my spirit, all the while doing something on the surface as different as enjoying a child's birthday party. I did not have to be consistent in the sense of having the same emotion throughout. Each part of me could entertain a separate experience all at once! Thus I could giggle in "joy inexpressible and full of glory" (1 Pet. 1:8) in one level of my spirit while fully borne down and silently sobbing with Jesus over recalcitrant Jerusalem in another, while playing a game with my children.

I know from prayer ministry experiences how desperately many Christians, both burden bearers and others, need to learn this lesson. Countless Christians suffer personal condemnation because they think something must be wrong with them when they want to laugh and cry at the same moment! In John 11, Jesus entered Bethany knowing He would raise Lazarus. He had already told the disciples His intention, two days beforehand (vv. 1–5). His spirit must have been rejoicing in anticipation of the great miracle He was to accomplish, for Lazarus' sake if for nothing else. But in front of the tomb, identifying in empathetic burden bearing with Martha and all the people, He wept (v. 35). We do not have to be consistent, only Christian! We are able to feel many things in many levels of our being, all at once.

Burden bearers need friends who watch over them to see when they are falling into the flesh, taking on too much too long, or too little too briefly. We need to help one another, to encourage one another (Phil. 2:1, 3), to look out "for the interests of others" (Phil. 2:4), to lift one another up (Eccles. 4:9–12), and to supply to one another (Eph. 4:16). In short, no burden bearer (in fact, no Christian anywhere) should ever serve alone.

Mainly, we need the hugs of Christian friends and relatives. Physical touch resonates. As one tuning fork can be struck and another chimes, so Christians restore one another to right keys and tones by touch. Paula restores me to who I am when the burdens of eighty people fill my heart and threaten to overwhelm and confuse my identity. A friend's pat on the shoulder may be sufficient, or a knowing look of empathy. We need to drink balance and give refreshment among friends.

LEECHES

The opposite of this balance and of what it is to be a burden bearer is being what we call a leech. Leeches are like vampires. They are already virtually dead. They sustain themselves by drinking the blood (energy) of others. They operate in the night (in the darkness of misunderstandings and hatred of self). They cannot stand the light of day (revelations of their own sins). They cannot stand mirrors (reflections of their own self and their sin).

Leeches attach themselves to people who have life in Jesus but who have not yet learned to die to the need to be needed. Leeches fasten onto people who need to have a ministry, who have not yet reckoned their gifting as their Isaac and sacrificed it on the altar. People who are more mature, who have died to self-importance and sacrificed their Isaacs, quickly discern and avoid the tentacles of leeches. They do not continue to give where the Lord does not.

In the early years of our ministry, Paula and I became surrounded and nearly borne down by spiritual leeches. These were weak people who liked to be dependent. They always had another emotional problem to be dealt with, another runny nose to wipe. They could latch onto us because we had not yet learned to say no. We were still pleased in our flesh that someone needed us. It made us feel important and successful to have people around us who hung on our words and asked us questions that made us feel wise and competent.

Hugs usually make one feel comforted, refreshed, or fulfilled. Hugging a leech leaves one feeling drained. These people are like vacuum cleaners, only they suck out the cleanness rather than the dirt! It seems as though burden bearers become filled with leeches' dirt to no avail. It would be OK, indeed our purpose, if, like St. Paul, death could be at work in us but life in them (2 Cor. 4:12). With leeches, it doesn't seem to do any good. Leeches feel better, but only momentarily. No life seems to be working in them. They fail to take hold and run on their own batteries.

Again it was Winston Nunes who set me free. We had been reading many works by Watchman Nee, especially *The Latent Power of the Soul*,[2] and had come to see that much of our ministry was only soulish striving and that truly "the flesh profits nothing" (John 6:63). But we didn't know how to get out of it. It was Winston who said, "John, your ministry is your Isaac. God wants you to sacrifice it."

Having accepted Winston as a man of God, I obeyed, little comprehending what I was doing. Afterward I saw that so long as a man holds any gift or talent, he and his soulish flesh, rather than

God, manipulate it. It possesses and drives him, rather than God possessing both it and him. Winston led me through the prayer of renunciation as an Abraham surrendering his Isaac. And he explained to me the meaning of Luke 14:26, that every skill in us is as our child, which is still permeated by our flesh, coated in the old wineskin. We must turn to hate even the garment spotted by the flesh (Jude 23) and bring to death on the cross everything in us— or it, rather than Jesus, will possess and control us.

The moment Winston led me through that prayer and I shared it with Paula, our need to be needed died. *Our* ministry died in that moment. Therefore we did not need hangers-on to convince us of the supposed worth of our ministry. It took discipline to learn to activate discernment. It took awhile to learn to say no. In the process we learned that unwittingly we had not been living for Jesus only, but for the ministry, using Jesus to further our ministry. When that died and we let that go, our security was again in Jesus, not in how well the ministry seemed to be going.

That meant that we were no longer blind to the leeches. We didn't have to do anything. Their blood supply dried up because we no longer poured out our own being to them, thinking it was Jesus. They just naturally wandered off to find others who had not developed the discernment to recognize leeches. A few of those who were leeches, finding the false supply shut down, turned and found their source and transformation in Christ.

As the body of Christ, as His burden bearers, we need to comprehend this aspect, actually the limit, to burden bearing, as in Galatians 6:5, "For each one shall bear his own load." Understanding it, we need to pray the Abraham-Isaac prayer. Sometimes I have felt led to add, "Now, Lord, we close all those inner doors that have been too open and loose from ourselves the spirits of all those who have latched onto us. Lord, seal up our inner being so that none may find wrong access to us again."

Unless one has become as crushed and overburdened as have some of us unwise, uncrucified, natural burden bearers, he cannot fully appreciate the blessed relief and release that such understanding and prayer afford! Let pastors examine their most faithfully serving sheep. So many servants have tragically burned out who need not have been lost had we understood the lesson of Abraham and Isaac!

We need not only to be taught to pray and release, but we also need to heal. We ought to allow the balm of the Lord to pour over us into all those overtired, overtaxed areas of our inner being, those areas that were not protected by enough wisdom and self-death.

It is not necessary to mount our charger to chase all the leeches out of the flock. God may use leeches to bring His servants to sufficient disgust to quit the self-filled game of ministry. And some of the leeches may find true faith. Let us only watch to minister to the Lord's servants such relief as we ourselves have found when we died to the need to be needed.

We close this chapter on burden bearing here, for only those who have learned the secret that God needs no one are safe to continue the hazards of burden-bearing ministry. We are not going to be allowed to retain a handle on God. He loves us all. And in the sense that every father needs every one of his children, God "needs" us. But in no other sense does He need us. When it comes to doing His ministry, He could replace us by another in a moment. He alone is God. He will not share His glory with another—for our sakes. It is not good to base a relationship solely on need. All need-based relationships are unstable. The world wants handles. It wants to be needed. Christians are free. They are not needed, but oh, so loved and wanted. They are free to give and receive love without making anyone dependent. Whoever thinks his church—or anyone, for that matter—cannot get along without him is in for a rude surprise. Let's learn to resign the general managership of the universe. It's quite a shock—and then fun— to discover how well family and friends, and the whole world, can get along without us! If we discover that, God may let the world need us because we don't need it, and neither we nor they will fall to idolatry. Here, as everywhere, death is the key to life.

CHAPTER 9

FITTING IN TO THE BODY OF CHRIST

Now there are varieties of gifts, but the same Spirit. And there are varieties of ministries, and the same Lord. And there are varieties of effects, but the same God who works all things in all persons. *But to each one is given the manifestation of the Spirit for the common good....* But now God has placed the members, each one of them, in the body, just as He desired. And if they were all one member, where would the body be? But now there are many members, but one body.... And if one member suffers, all the members suffer with it; if one member is honored, all the members rejoice with it. Now you are Christ's body, and individually members of it.

—1 CORINTHIANS 12:4–27, EMPHASIS ADDED

From whom the whole body, being fitted and held together by that which every joint supplies, according to the proper working of each individual part, causes the growth of the body for the building up of itself in love.

—EPHESIANS 4:16

The body of Christ is not yet fully functioning as a living organism. Right now it more likely resembles a two-year-old's collage—toes stuck gleefully to the head, fingers protruding from the heel, and eyes popping out from the navel. Or we could be compared to multitudes of fish swimming in the same bowl, largely unaware of relevance or duty to one another. This is true whether we speak of members within one local church, of churches in a denomination, or of independent churches and denominations in the body.

What remains to be defeated is individualism—not individualism in itself, for we will always need and cherish strong individuals—but the corporate stronghold that isolates and idolizes. The corporate stronghold of privacy now prevents that depth of sharing that alone can awaken the churches.

> Arise, shine; for your light has come,
> And the glory of the LORD has risen upon you.
> For behold, darkness will cover the earth,
> And deep darkness the peoples;
> But the LORD will rise upon you,
> And His glory will appear upon you.
> And nations will come to your light,
> And kings to the brightness of your rising.
>
> —ISAIAH 60:1–3

The Word will not fail to bring forth (Isa. 55:11). The Church will arise.

> In the last days,
> The mountain of the house of the LORD
> Will be established as the chief of the mountains,
> And will be raised above the hills;

And all the nations will stream to it.
And many peoples will come and say,
"Come, let us go up to the mountain of the LORD,
To the house of the God of Jacob;
That He may teach us concerning His ways,
And that we may walk in His paths."
For the law will go forth from Zion.
And the word of the LORD from Jerusalem.

—ISAIAH 2:2–3

If Isaiah spoke as we believe in vision of these latter days and of the Church, then this word prophesies of the new. "Zion" is His gathered and prepared people, and so is "Jerusalem." That means that the "law" that will go forth from Zion is not the Old Testament, nor is it the Ten Commandments or the Torah. It is the New, not even the Sermon on the Mount, but the commandment of Jesus: "A new commandment I give unto you, That ye love one another; *as* I have loved you" (John 13:34, KJV, emphasis added). How did He love us? By laying down his life for us. "Bear ye one another's burdens, and so fulfil *the law of Christ*" (Gal. 6:2, KJV, emphasis added). That is the law that will go forth, not as a law passed by a senate, but as a way of life written in the heart and acted among men by every Christian.

> In that day shall the branch of the LORD be beautiful and glorious, and the fruit of the earth shall be excellent and comely for them that are escaped of Israel. And it shall come to pass, that he that is left in Zion, and he that remaineth in Jerusalem, shall be called holy, even every one that is written among the living in Jerusalem: When the Lord shall have washed away the filth of the daughters of Zion, and shall have purged the blood of Jerusalem from the midst thereof by

the spirit of judgment, and by the spirit of burning. And the
LORD will create upon every dwelling place of mount Zion,
and upon her assemblies, a cloud and smoke by day, and the
shining of a flaming fire by night: for upon all the glory shall
be a defence. And there shall be a tabernacle for a shadow in
the daytime from the heat, and for a place of refuge, and for a
covert from storm and from rain.

—ISAIAH 4:2–6, KJV

The Shekinah glory of God will again rest over God's people,
this time not only over the tabernacle ("her assemblies") as in the
wilderness, but also over "every dwelling place," meaning over
every home of every Christian! Each and every one in the Church
will be called holy. When? "When the Lord shall have washed away
the filth…by the spirit of judgment, and by the spirit of burning."
That means that the fullness of power waits upon one thing—the
coming of the spirit of judgment and burning. That very thing is
prophesied as the task of God's "messenger."

"Behold, I am going to send My messenger, and he will clear the
way before Me. And the Lord, whom you seek, will suddenly
come to His temple; and the messenger of the covenant, in
whom you delight, behold, He is coming," says the LORD of
hosts. "But who can endure the day of His coming? And who
can stand when He appears? For he is like a refiner's fire and
like fullers' soap. And He will sit as a smelter and purifier of
silver, and He will purify the sons of Levi and refine them like
gold and silver, so that they may present to the LORD offerings
in righteousness. Then the offering of Judah and Jerusalem
will be pleasing to the LORD, as in the days of old and as in
former years. Then I will draw near to you for judgment; and
I will be a swift witness against the sorcerers and against the
adulterers and against those who swear falsely, and against

those who oppress the wage earner in his wages, the widow and the orphan, and those who turn aside the alien, and do not fear Me," says the LORD of hosts.

—MALACHI 3:1–5

"For behold, the day is coming, burning like a furnace; and all the arrogant and every evildoer will be chaff; and the day that is coming will set them ablaze," says the LORD of hosts, "so that it will leave them neither root nor branch. But for you who fear My name the sun of righteousness will rise with healing in its wings; and you will go forth and skip about like calves from the stall. And you will tread down the wicked, for they shall be ashes under the soles of your feet on the day which I am preparing," says the LORD of hosts.

"Remember the law of Moses My servant, even the statutes and ordinances which I commanded him in Horeb for all Israel. Behold, I am going to send you Elijah the prophet before the coming of the great and terrible day of the LORD. And he will restore the hearts of the fathers to their children, and the hearts of the children to their fathers, lest I come and smite the land with a curse."

—MALACHI 4:1–6

The Church does not exist for itself. Its glory is not to bask in God's presence, although that is our joy and His joy, to have His sons and daughters in fellowship with Him. Rather, its glory is in being that "shadow in the daytime from the heat, and for a place of refuge, and for a covert from storm and from rain" (Isa. 4:6, KJV). God does not intend to jerk His own out of the world so He can beat up on everyone who hasn't received Him. It is the exact opposite! He sees the increasing wickedness of mankind and knows the holocausts He must send in reaping for what we have sown. Therefore, "God so hated the world that He pulled the Son out of it"—shame on mankind for ever perverting a proper under-standing of God's Word and of His nature! No! "God so loved the world, that He gave His only begotten Son..." (John 3:16). He is still sending the Son, that when men reap the horrible destructions they so richly deserve, His Church may be there, in the midst of tribulation, to spread a canopy of defense, to be an umbrella of protection, a mother hen under which the frightened chicks of the world can run for cover!

God is raising up a remnant to stand, prepared and victorious, an army of light in a darkened world. That presages a definitive, learned, and achieved lifestyle—a people who have become disciplined to live Christ regularly, as instinctively as breathing, for the welfare of others. What God wants is a transformed people, through whom the sacrificial life of Jesus is as normal as flowers reaching for sunlight.

Many Christians yearn for the lifestyle without paying the price of disciplined effort to learn and grow: "I accepted Jesus, and suddenly my life was changed" is the testimony heard again and again in the Christian media and at inspirational banquets. Such claims need some translation. "Suddenly" Jesus's power is available for transformation, but real change is always only sustained by multitudes of subsequent little choices and deliberate acting upon them:

> Even so consider yourselves to be dead to sin, but alive to God in Christ Jesus. Therefore do not let sin reign in your mortal body that you should obey its lusts, and do not go on presenting the members of your body to sin as instruments of unrighteousness; but present yourselves to God as those alive from the dead, and your members as instruments of righteousness to God.
>
> —ROMANS 6:11–13, EMPHASIS ADDED

When we have prayed for and received forgiveness, when we have in prayer brought the power of an old habit structure to death on the cross, the old way has no more claim upon us. However, it may have some power to allure and grab us because: (1) we have so long practiced that habitual way of thinking, of feeling, and of acting that it is the easiest way to go, causing us to slide into the familiar groove without thinking; and (2) Satan would love to entice or push us to act out the proverb, "Like a dog that returns to its vomit is a fool who repeats his folly" (Prov. 26:11). That means that each time we are tempted to act in the sinful way from which we have been set free, we have the power by the presence of Jesus in us to stop and to make a choice. "I recognize that I am tempted [for instance] to respond with an outburst of temper. Lord, I'd really like to belt that guy! I know where that old habit started [often in childhood]. Thank You, Lord, that I have been set free by the blood of Jesus. That old habit no longer has the right or power to control and drive me. I renounce it. I will not respond in the old way. Come, Lord Jesus; let Your living presence within me supply me with a wise and loving answer to the present irritation." Especially when we are newly set free, the choosing of the new way may involve some struggle, but as we persist, the new way will gradually become that which automatically flows from us as a trained-in habit pattern. We will always retain enough of the struggle to keep us aware that without Jesus we can do nothing (John 15:5).

The irritations that trigger our old habit patterns are not always easily recognizable. They are often like sneaky little foxes slipping in to eat our tender grapes.

Catch the foxes for us,
The little foxes that are ruining the vineyards,
While our vineyards are in blossom.

—SONG OF SOLOMON 2:15

In Bible lands, when a field was planted, a hedge was put about that field to protect it from invasion by small, hungry animals. A booth was erected on stilts in the midst of the field, and a boy was hired to watch for intruders. Spotting an animal breaking through the hedge, the boy would hurl a stone with his slingshot in an attempt to frighten away the potential attacker. Or he would descend from his high perch to chase away or to catch and throw out the more persistent ones.

In the same way, there are foxes of thought that can creep through our mental and emotional defenses to threaten the development of the new fruit of the garden of our life as it begins to blossom in us. A reformed alcoholic may take just a little nip to relax his nerves before encountering that next, most-important client. A healed homosexual may return to former associates too soon in his zeal to help. A person may indulge in a bit of fantasizing in loneliness and fall prey to an old pattern of self-pity or to the enticement of a relationship that wrongly promises comfort. Any one of us may indulge in a short flash of anger (because "they deserve it" or "they have to learn not to walk on people") and soon find ourselves overwhelmed and carried away by our emotional outburst. Any acceptance or expression of "just a little won't hurt," when the tender grapes of our new life are still in fragile blossom, leaves us wide open to the taking over of our garden by little foxes who will greedily devour our promises of new life and grow thereby to be big foxes who rule the garden before we have experienced much harvest of fruit in our lives.

It is for this reason that we read such passages from the Scriptures:

> *We have not ceased to pray for you* and to ask that you may be filled with the knowledge of His will in all spiritual wisdom and understanding, so that you may *walk in a manner worthy of the Lord*, to please Him in all respects, *bearing fruit* in every good work and *increasing* in the knowledge of God; *strengthened* with all power, according to His glorious might, for *the attaining of all steadfastness* and patience, joyously giving thanks to the Father, who has qualified us to share in the inheritance of the saints in light.
> —COLOSSIANS 1:9–12, EMPHASIS ADDED

As you therefore have received Christ Jesus the Lord, *so walk in Him,* having been *firmly rooted* and *now being built up* in Him and *established* in your faith, just as you were instructed, and overflowing with gratitude. *See to it* that no one takes you captive through philosophy and empty deception.

—COLOSSIANS 2:6–8, EMPHASIS ADDED
(SEE ALSO EPHESIANS 2:10; 4:1; 1 THESSALONIANS 2:12)

We are called to live and grow in a healthful balance of *resting* in the Lord with a sure knowledge of the fact that it is not by might, not by power, but by the Lord's Spirit that we accomplish anything (Zech. 4:6), *coupled with very active, moment-by-moment discipline:*

- "*Conduct yourselves* with wisdom" (Col. 4:5).

- "*Let* your speech always be seasoned with grace" (Col. 4:6).

- "*Let* the peace of Christ rule in your hearts...be thankful" (Col. 3:15).

- "*Do not be* embittered" (Col. 3:19).

- "*Be* obedient" (Col. 3:20).

- "*Do your work heartily*" (Col. 3:23).

- "*Examine* everything carefully" (1 Thess. 5:21).

- "*Abstain* from every form of evil" (1 Thess. 5:22).

- *"Fight the good fight* of faith; take hold of the eternal life to which you were called" (1 Tim. 6:12).

- *"Be diligent* to present yourself approved to God as a workman who does not need to be ashamed" (2 Tim. 2:15).

- *"Refuse* foolish and ignorant speculations" (2 Tim. 2:23).

- *"Continue* in the things you have learned" (2 Tim. 3:14).

- *"Endure* hardship" (2 Tim. 4:5).

- *"Do not speak against one another"* (James 4:11).

- *"Do not complain"* (James 5:9).

- *"Keep fervent* in your love for one another" (1 Pet. 4:8).

- *"...casting* all your anxiety on Him" (1 Pet. 5:7).

- *"Make* straight paths for your feet" (Heb. 12:13).

- *"Pursue peace* with all men" (Heb. 12:14).

- *"See to it*...that no root of bitterness springing up causes trouble" (Heb. 12:15).

- *"Keep* yourselves in the love of God" (Jude 21).

⊰ "...applying all *diligence*, in your faith supply moral excellence, and in your moral excellence, knowledge; and in your knowledge, *self-control*, and in your self-control, *perseverance*, and in your perseverance, godliness; and in your godliness, brotherly kindness, and in your brotherly kindness, love" (2 Pet. 1:5–7).

All of these scriptures of discipline possess one basic motif: they are all meant to establish and maintain the life of Jesus in us. That life is His life of giving us to others for their sake. Such a life creates humility, for it so often drives us against the stubborn walls of our yet-undead flesh that we see again and again our continual need of daily death and rebirth. We soon lose our willingness to judge others and feel superior, wondering how they can be gracious when we so often can't.

> Do nothing out of selfish ambition or vain conceit, but in humility consider others better than yourselves. Each of you should look not only to your own interests, but also to the interests of others.
> —PHILIPPIANS 2:3–4, NIV

When self is finally overcome (and what more appropriately than self can Jesus be mentioning as a constant refrain as something that needs to be overcome in Revelation 2:7, 11, 17, 26; 3:5, 12, 21), then the body will be one constant light of love poured out for the sake of mankind and all the heavens as God intended.

> Although I am less than the least of all God's people, this grace was given me: to preach to the Gentiles the unsearchable riches of Christ, and to make plain to everyone the administration of this mystery, which for ages past was

kept hidden in God, who created all things. His intent was that now, through the church, the manifold wisdom of God should be made known to the rulers and authorities in the heavenly realms, according to his eternal purpose which he accomplished in Christ Jesus our Lord.

—EPHESIANS 3:8–11, NIV

The end of transformation is not a few scattered individuals who shine as sparks running through the stubble (Isa. 47:14). It is an army of fire blazing a pathway of mercy. No one is fully transformed who does not yet know himself to be one tiniest portion of the body of Christ. Ephesians 4:16 says that we are to be "fitted and held together by that which every joint supplies, according to the proper working of each individual part." As each transforming individual contributes that unique glory (1 Cor. 12:14–20) God created him to be, our joining supplies to each of us what we need from one another, as all are held together by love. That supply mutually equips, and the body upbuilds. We need one another. No man is complete alone.

However significant any man's contribution may be, the warfare is that of an army, and the victory is that of the Lord of hosts.

The fullness of transformation means that we will no longer have to think to remind ourselves that we are an army. We will no longer have to work to establish teamwork. We will no longer have to struggle against the self that isolates, nor will we have to fear domination and control. Oneness will be our most natural and easy ground (Ps. 133), and blessedness will roll down like a mighty river. The purpose of transformation is to bring us to that point in which unity of faith has succeeded unity of the Spirit (Eph. 4:3–13) and in which truth sparks responses in love and laughter and all enhance each to fullness—without sweat and strain. The home of each soul is the company of the faithful. And home is the place of rest. We shall know when we are departing from oneness by the recurrence of striving, and we shall laughingly and easily return by the door of grace.

Transformation is not the end product. It is the process by which we get there. Transformation proceeds within each individual by the presence and power of the Lord mainly through the company of Christ, but its purpose is not solely to present individuals without spot or wrinkle before the Father (Eph. 5:27), but a body, one in all its holy motives and desires. "That he might present it to himself a glorious church, not having spot, or wrinkle, or any such thing; but that it should be holy and without blemish" (Eph. 5:27, KJV).

Transformation struggles in the beginning by leaps and bounds (and pitfalls) from crag to crag of knowledge and revelation, but it is simple fellowship that walks us in the end across a level plain of rejoicing into the hall of the marriage feast! It is fellowship that graces the heart with possibility for living in heavenly repose and response. It is fellowship that sings a song to tired hearts and sparks resurrection of skills first planted by God and long forgotten by men. It is fellowship that strikes hands and lifts loads far beyond one alone. It is fellowship that finally enables forgetting of what lies behind and makes possible pressing forward to the mark of the prize of the high calling of God in Christ Jesus (Phil 3:13–14).

In the end it shall be a chorus, not a solo. And we shall all find a voice that no longer creaks and cracks; carried in embrace we shall find it easy to stand in judgment without being fearful.

> By this, love is perfected with us, that we may have confidence in the day of judgment; because as He is, so also are we in this

world. There is no fear in love; but perfect love casts out fear, because fear involves punishment, and the one who fears is not perfected in love. We love, because He first loved us.

—1 JOHN 4:17–19

Obeying the command to "remember all the way which the LORD your God has led you in the wilderness these forty years" (Deut. 8:2) shall no longer be a disgrace but the prelude and vast fount out of which our wisdom arises (Matt. 11:25) to rule the many things over which God places His own in the kingdom (Matt. 25:21–23).

The end of transformation is rule, but not as solitary kings and queens; rather, it is as a company of the faithful, lovingly cherishing what each gives to each.

NOTES

CHAPTER 1—GROWING UP AGAIN—IN CHRIST

1. John Loren and Paula Sandford, *The Elijah Task* (Lake Mary, FL: 2006).

CHAPTER 3—FINDING IDENTITY AND CALLING

1. William Ernest Henley, "Invictus," as viewed at Bartleby.com, http://www.bartleby.com/103/7.html (accessed August 20, 2007).

CHAPTER 6—TOWARD SEXUAL WHOLENESS: BECOMING CHRISTLIKE IN OUR HUMANNESS

1. United Nations Population Fund, "A Human Rights and Health Priority," *The State of the World Population 2000*, http://www.unfpa.org/swp/2000/english/ch03.html (accessed September 10, 2007).

CHAPTER 7—OVERCOMING GENDER IDENTITY ISSUES

1. Thomas Verny, MD, *The Secret Life of the Unborn Child* (New York: Dell Publishing, 1982).

2. John Loren Sandford, *Why Good People Mess Up* (Lake Mary, FL: Charisma House, 2007).

3. John Paul Jackson, *Needless Casualties of War* (North Sutton, NH: Streams Publishing House, 1999).

CHAPTER 8—HE'S NOT HEAVY—HE'S MY BROTHER

1. Walt Whitman, "Song of Myself," as viewed at University of Illinois–Urbana-Champaign, Department of English, http://www.english.uiuc.edu/maps/poets/s_z/whitman/song.htm (accessed September 11, 2007).

2. Watchman Nee, *The Latent Power of the Soul* (Richmond, VA: Christian Fellowship Publishers, 1972).

Other Books by John Loren and Paula Sandford

A Comprehensive Guide to Deliverance and Inner Healing

Awakening the Slumbering Spirit

Choosing Forgiveness

Elijah Among Us

God's Power to Change

Healing for a Woman's Emotions

Healing the Nations

Healing Victims of Sexual Abuse

Prophets, Healers and the Emerging Church

Renewal of the Mind

Restoring the Christian Family

The Elijah Task

Transforming the Inner Man

Why Good People Mess Up

For further information, contact:

Elijah House, Inc.

317 N. Pines Road

Spokane Valley, WA 99206

Web site: www.elijahhouse.org

The Road to Hope, Healing, and
Spiritual Growth Starts Here

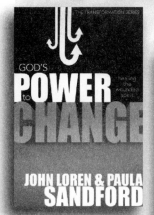

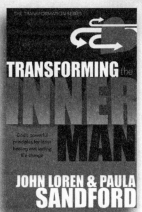

If you have been encouraged by *Letting Go of Your Past,* you will want to read books one and two of The Transformation Series.

A STRANG COMPANY

Transforming the Inner Man / 978-1-59979-067-1 / $14.99
Book One of The Transformation Series
Discover the steps for true, lasting change by learning how to break negative habits and eliminate the roots of habitual sins.

God's Power to Change / 978-1-59979-068-8 / $14.99
Book Two of The Transformation Series
This book presents the realities of wounds and sins that exist in your personal spirit and gives principles for awakening, repairing, and restoring your spirit into healing and wholeness.

The life you were created for is within your grasp!
Available where fine Christian books are sold.

Strang Communications,

publisher of both **Charisma House** and
Charisma magazine, wants to give you

3 FREE ISSUES
of our **award-winning** magazine.

WWW.CHARISMAMAG.COM

Since its inception in 1975, *Charisma* magazine has
helped thousands of Christians stay connected with
what God is doing worldwide.

Within its pages you will discover in-depth reports
and the latest news from a Christian perspective,
biblical health tips, global events in the body of Christ,
personality profiles, and so much more. Join the family
of *Charisma* readers who enjoy feeding their spirit
each month with miracle-filled testimonies and
inspiring articles that bring clarity, provoke
prayer, and demand answers.

To claim your **3 free issues** of *Charisma*,
send your name and address to:
Charisma 3 Free Issue Offer, 600
Rinehart Road, Lake Mary, FL 32746.
Or you may call **1-800-829-3346**
and ask for Offer **#97FREE**. This
offer is only valid in the USA.

Charisma
+CHRISTIAN LIFE
www.charismamag.com

7347